Contents

Preface

How to use this book

The aims of this little book are to provide a teacher with some lively descriptions of primary school science education in action; to express a theory and philosophy appropriate for primary science teaching at this time; and to give an uncertain teacher some hundreds of practical ideas for working successfully with young children at being 'simple scientists'. A good way to begin reading the book is to refer to one or two of the author's personal 'case histories', such as *The Clay Boat Project* (pages 43–51), and *Discovering Magnetism with Younger Juniors* (pages 52–60). After these pleasant excursions into the classroom, it would make sense to read and think about the section on *Questions of Primary Science* (pages 5–14), which is meant to reassure teachers that coping with science in the elementary curriculum is not the frightening task that some teachers, understandably, believe. The sections about key concepts give guidance on the sorts of content a science programme might have, and there is deeper advice on developing a science policy for an individual school. These latter sections will be especially useful for discussion, and as a basis of action, with staff 'science leaders' in schools, and with local science advisers on courses.

Throughout the book there are ideas, deliberately kept brief, and – wherever possible – requiring minimal preparation, which are intended to stimulate a teacher's imagination and creativity about what activities are possible with particular children. Most of the material in this book originally appeared in articles published in the journals *Teachers' World*, *Child Education*, *The School Science Review*, and *Science Activities* (USA) and has already proved itself to be of value to non-specialist teachers. Finally, the author wishes to thank Dr Wynne Harlen for her kindness in allowing her thoughts on curriculum content to be included.

Alan Ward

Cheltenham, 1983

A
Source Book for
Primary Science
Education

Alan Ward

HODDER AND STOUGHTON
LONDON SYDNEY AUCKLAND TORONTO

British Library Cataloguing in Publication Data

Ward, Alan, *1932*–
  A source book for primary science education.
  1. Science—study and teaching (Elementary)
  I. Title
  372.3'5044   LB1585

ISBN 0 340 33421 5

First published 1983

Printed and bound in Great Britain for
Hodder and Stoughton Educational,
a division of Hodder and Stoughton Ltd,
Mill Road, Dunton Green, Sevenoaks, Kent
by J. W. Arrowsmith Ltd, Bristol

Set in 11/12 point Plantin (Linotron) by
Rowland Phototypesetting Ltd, Bury St Edmunds, Suffolk.

Introduction

Primary school science is essentially an attitude to learning about the physical world and how it works. The attitude is expressed through acting and thinking in certain ways. These ways involve describing accurate first-hand observations, making measurements, doing simple tests to help answer questions, and trying to sort facts into patterns. A scientific fact is verifiable. This means that most people believe it because its truth can be confirmed by repeating the appropriate tests and observations. Historically, the scientific attitude has led to tremendous advances in everyday technology and material prosperity, which we all enjoy, but tend to take for granted. These advances rest upon the superb reliability of scientific knowledge.

If, therefore, we believe that the primary school curriculum should reflect everyday experiences, science cannot be neglected, because its influence is so powerful. But the real power of science does not exist in mere scientific things, like electric kettles and aeroplanes, but in the manner of scientific thinking, acting and believing. This is why nothing has so far been said about scientific concepts. Young children are likely to be interested in nature, their own bodies, raw materials, structures, air, water, and in everything that moves. These topics can all be covered in their routine lessons. If the topics are treated scientifically, children should acquire basic scientific concepts automatically. The great need is to reveal the physical world through a scientific approach, without destroying a child's sense of mystery and wonder.

Teachers and, indeed, parents need to be convinced about the value to children of what is taught. Then a teacher may act with a feeling of commitment, and a parent may be reassured that what education the school offers makes practical good sense. That is why it is essential to think about the reasons why certain subjects and particular ideas are included in the curriculum. Teaching science in the primary school seems a new idea to many people, but this is not so, because there is a long tradition of teaching science to infants and juniors through nature study.

Furthermore, science has been taught 'accidentally' through other subjects: for example, weather studies and compass work in geography, and through such topics as the ever popular 'Story of Flight and Flying Machines'. The new idea about primary science teaching is to focus less on facts or concepts for their own sake and more on the activities of scientific finding out, decision-making, problem-solving and logical thinking.

But what are the reasons for taking science seriously in primary schools? Nature study remains an important part of the work. However, there can be no denying that we find ourselves in an environment that is shaped and maintained by the applied science called technology. Especially if we live in a city, we are dependent upon technology for well-being and survival. What would happen if, suddenly, all water, gas and electricity services ceased to function? Even the ways we think about society and the behaviour of individual human beings are influenced by scientific attitudes. Scientific thinking is also needed to help us to solve crucial problems about the earth's limited physical and living resources and sources of energy, in a world where still-growing populations are demanding better living standards.

Children are interested in their environment. Learning about their surroundings is therefore relevant learning. In a techno-logical world this will mean wanting to know about technical things, as well as about nature – so primary school teachers cannot avoid making the whole field of science a potential source for activities. Science helps people to use technology sensibly and to have some understanding of how things work. This means taking note of the physical sciences, which have not previously been thought very significant for primary school children. Scientific work ranging over all such areas can be as exciting as nature study, and the subject-matter will help teachers to provide interesting and stimulating work in connec-tion with the high priority work in literacy and numeracy.

Unfortunately there are difficulties in persuading all primary school teachers that they can include much scientific work in their teaching programmes. Some of the difficulties are psycho-logical, but none the less real for that. Not all people find it natural or easy to think in ways that scientists are reputed to do, and a minority of teachers may even refuse to try. The negative image of science is associated with tediously precise and dif-ficult explanations, and with the horrors of modern warfare, ecological damage and pollution. If teachers who have a low aptitude for science, or active prejudice against it, would take the trouble to observe how much interest and pleasure the most straightforward scientific activities give to children, those teachers may be led to favour the subject more.

Then there are teachers who feel that their alleged lack of scientific knowledge and training disqualify them from taking it seriously in the classroom. If only they would understand that real science is about thinking and acting in certain ways, perhaps they could begin to learn the facts alongside children who are engaged in appropriate investigations, such as learning to associate cloud shapes with weather patterns, or building model arches with wedge-shaped blocks, in order to appreciate how 'keystones' work in ancient bridge and church structures.

Another difficulty occurs when a teacher who has a good scientific background finds it hard to think and act at a young child's intellectual level. Other teachers have a real fear of having to answer children's questions about science. Ironically, this fear is largely a phantom one, because children ask few questions on any subject to which simple, albeit superficial answers cannot be given by an imaginative teacher. If a teacher feels able to be an authority on most routine subject-matter covered by the curriculum, there is no need to be ashamed of admitting ignorance sometimes. Children appreciate honesty. The reader may be assured that the author appreciates these difficulties which teachers do feel. This book will be an attempt to alleviate worries and fears about primary science. The book also contains practical advice and guidance, aimed at helping non-specialist primary school teachers to accomplish some elementary science work cheerfully and effectively.

The book begins with an outline of the author's own divergent ideas about the presentation of science in the primary school. These ideas are expressed in the form of extended answers to questions that are typical of those asked by teachers. Perhaps the hardest question to answer, and yet the most interesting one, is how to evaluate the results of spontaneous investigations – those not merely prescribed or done to illustrate directly taught facts.

Attention will be paid to the sorts of scientific concepts that children of primary school age may be expected to meet and understand. The concepts are accompanied by many ideas for learning activities. This section of the book can be dipped into as a source book within a source book. Teaching methods are illustrated through case histories based on the author's work in schools. An 'Ideas Bank' provides another section consisting of many briefly described ideas intended to stimulate as well as assist the reader's thinking. Advice is given on the writing of a primary school science policy, and there are reflections on the style of primary school science as opposed to secondary approaches. The book ends with suggestions on what materials need be bought, and there is a short but comprehensive bibliography of books that will give the user value for money.

I
Questions of Primary Science: important questions which have been asked by teachers, with some practical answers

Primary science for beginners

I know that science is important – but how do I start organising lessons with the forty-two children in my class?

It might be helpful to put aside the myth that so-called child-centredness is the only way to angle successful lessons. By successful, I mean learning experiences that draw an interested response from the class. The most convenient way to monitor such a reaction is to have exciting dialogue in depth, involving *all* the children. It is incumbent upon the good teacher to master the art of organising knowledge and information, through skilful and stimulating questioning.

Writing simple work cards on a topic such as 'Sound' is a practical way to introduce children to interesting scientific material. Time spent browsing in a bookshop reveals several little books written directly for children, giving instructions for easy experiments improvised from 'junk' materials such as yogurt pots and rubber bands. Superior children's books contain everything the beginning teacher needs to know. An apt author's choice of wording is an inspiration for the teacher's task of translating technical information into language children will understand.

Time given to composing work cards and collecting 'kits' of apparatus is well spent if the end products are to be used and adapted many times. Only the teacher can judge which words will be appropriate, though commercially produced cards can serve as time-saving models of what to do. Don't overcrowd the cards. Take trouble to form and arrange the wording to give it visual appeal. Perhaps the local Teachers' Centre has a typewriter with big letter faces. Experiment with different wording and simple illustrations, until the meaning is clear to the children. Assemble the kits of cards and apparatus for class work, in trays improvised from shirt boxes (obtainable free from men's clothes shops).

Ten working groups, each of four children, will probably be the maximum possible in a crowded classroom containing forty pupils. In such a case, work might proceed on a basis of a circus of five (duplicated) activities. All five should occupy the children for no longer than two hour-long periods, in consecutive weeks. With experience, a teacher can modify activities to take roughly equal times, so that all the children are active. For the occasional activity – like making a yogurt pot telephone – space outside the room is essential. If preferred, recording can be limited to ongoing discussion with groups, followed by full class discussion when the happenings are over. Many teachers find the circus approach hectic because, in fact, several lessons are going on all at once. It is less wearing on nerves to have every group doing say two activities per lesson – always followed by class discussion, limited to the particular topics covered.

I generally encourage primary children to write and draw about what they do and find out. Then I examine the children's efforts, before editing the best 'bits' by cutting out and pasting together a class record. In time, even the least communicative child produces an interesting picture or sentence to enhance the record, so everybody contributes.

A more formal, but still useful, approach to primary science teaching is by way of the class lesson, *but with individual children participating in experiments, on behalf of their classmates*. I have watched a student present a lesson about 'Dissolving substances' with her materials set out upon a slightly raised table, in front of a tightly-packed classroom. As discussion of the topic continued, boys and girls took turns to go up and do various tests. The well-behaved children evidently enjoyed the lesson, which the student conducted in the manner of a cheerful conjuror at a children's party, though it was clear that she was selling science, not magic.

Success with such teaching greatly depends upon the teacher's ability to programme the questioning, to keep the children thinking. A teacher could begin by asking what mother would do if Jimmy tipped ink over the tablecloth, or how oil stains can be removed from clothing. A teacher should be quick to exploit any gratuitous anecdotes offered by the children. 'Our Mum cleans our Dad's cricket trousers with meths . . .' Dissolving sugar cubes are dramatic to watch, as gradually the lumps crumble into heaps. *Such displays should be raised on a box, where every child can follow what is happening.* My student went on to organise crystal-growing in dishes which the children could inspect daily.

A teacher who has gained confidence in the ability to handle science topics might feel able to tackle a more open-ended theme: for example, a study of waste ground near the school. Groups of children could map the area, survey the native plants and 'minibeasts' (woodlice, tiger beetles, striped snails and hunting spiders . . .). Even rubbish is interesting, and clearing the plot of scrap will be a token act of environmental improvement. Survey the variety of rubbish found. What metals? Can old machinery be identified? How many sorts of used bricks? *Drawings and descriptions from life, and a collection of specimen items and creatures, will fascinate other children.*

Perhaps the teacher – now an enthusiast – will feel able to graduate from this approach to more extended studies, such as those pioneered by important science curriculum projects, such as the Schools Council *Science 5/13*. For grander themes, such as structures and forces in bridge construction, or an investigation of the properties of metals, it is desirable to timetable longer time blocks, to accommodate necessarily slower, more child-centred and original work. Nevertheless, teachers who feel that they cannot (yet) aspire to this type of organisation, need not feel ashamed if they are doing their utmost to bring thought-provoking, interesting science activities to the children.

The key to scientific activity is the habit of investigation. Taking a census of traffic is a popular mathematical exercise. It is also practical science – an attempt to answer the question: What are the proportions of lorries, buses and cars passing the school? It can lead to other questions. How can we find out where the lorries come from? How many vehicles break the speed limit? Children observing autumnal leaf-fall, before creative writing, can notice the abundance of various yellows, reds and browns in the colours, find words to describe how the branches move, and reflect upon nature's recycling of resources, when the leaves decay on the wet ground.

Science begins when we notice something interesting, and ask a question about it. Why are there snails on those old eggshells? Can all woodlice roll themselves, armadillo-like, into pea-size balls? How many young can a greenfly conceive in an afternoon? How many different lichens grow on the wall? What is the prevailing wind around the school? How much (by weight) of rubbish does the caretaker remove from the waste-paper baskets in a week? *Science is a rich source of interesting practical material upon which to base development of communication and number skills.* As there is no science syllabus, work can be original and unhurried.

Juniors studying the structure of insects, by doing large painstaking drawings from living specimens, needed little persuasion to measure the creatures in millimetres, before stating beneath their pictures just how much bigger than life-size the drawings were. Simon – a boy of 'below average ability' – produced remarkably accurate impressions of beetles. Science was a way for Simon to exploit his flair purposefully. And class discussion on forces, weight and volume stimulated another 'dull' boy to do much-improved written work. *These children were also acquiring attitudes of value for when science is taught more formally* in later school years.

'How much can a fist push aside?' Young juniors took turns at submerging their clenched hands to the wrist in a jar of water marked in centimetres up its side. Standard units of volume were not used, because the children were still merely approaching the volume concept. However, the technique gave data for graphically representing comparative fist displacements of the water. Did the children realise that the results also showed relative fist sizes? This would emerge from discussion. But the activity embodied concrete experience of notions about volume and displacement. *Simple practical science of this sort provides plenty of scope for conceptual education.*

Infants, using an inverted water-filled sweet jar, standing in a big bowl of water, were investigating how much air their lungs could hold. Stuart blew the air up into the jar through a plastic tube, after taking a deep breath. Then he took a second breath, and began blowing into the pipe again. Several children objected that he was cheating . . . So the test was repeated. When the proper quantity of air had displaced some water in the jar – to give an *impression* of the body's capacity – we put a rubber band around the jar, to mark the water level. Jason, watching the operation attentively, was most particular about where the band was put. *Science provides practice in critical thinking.*

Scientific observation is a more impressive and effective way of acquiring knowledge than mere book-learning, because it engages curiosity, stimulates the senses, and captures the imagination. Infants, basing much of their work on the theme of water, studied waterproofing, floating and sinking, water wheels and even model steam-engines. Hanging up in the room was a huge inflated plastic globe. Suddenly some children, in looking at the globe, realised that most of the world was covered with sea. It was a real discovery, not taught directly by the teacher. But the clever teacher was responsible for 'discovery potential' in the classroom environment.

Why we teach primary science

Science is a secondary school subject, too difficult for young children; furthermore, few primary teachers feel qualified to teach it, so why attempt scientific activities with infants and juniors?
I don't blame teachers who thus protest, when ambitious colleagues and enthusiastic educationists recommend that science be slotted into an already overcrowded schedule of subjects, including the priority obligation to impart basic skills of reading, writing and mathematics to forty children of widely-ranging abilities and home backgrounds. In a climate of rapid educational and social change, once-confident effective teachers feel pressured and unsure.

I propose to show that science is no novelty in primary schools – and often in the very rooms – where these justly unhappy teachers work. It need not be an added subject burden. Aspects of scientific education will already be included under the banners of familiar subject names. To adopt the additional role of part-time science teacher, it is sufficient to recognise 'scientific potential' in workaday situations. When common birds are visiting the school bird table, it is not even necessary to know much about the birds in order to ask the children to notice if all the birds take the crumbs in the same way.

Watching together, the teacher and the children discover that blue tits fly with their bread to a nearby tree, where they eat by gripping the food against a branch with their feet while pecking at leisure. Meanwhile, starlings gulp the crumbs in a seemingly greedy way, and a robin flies off with its small share to eat in private. *Both teacher and the children are becoming experts on ways birds feed in a garden.* The children have exciting discoveries to write about, and incentives to read more about birds in books, while the teacher is wondering whether the class can make a graph, showing mathematically which birds visit the bird table most or least.

Emphasis on the process

I don't think I could teach science. Nature study is no bother. But real science frightens me.

With thoughts such as these, many primary teachers immunise themselves against the friendly onslaughts of science advisers. Mrs Thompson confessed her fear of 'real science' (by which she meant elementary physics), but later she told me about a wonderful field trip she had organised, to a local farm. Her class watched cows being milked, learned the number of eggs hens could lay in a week, and questioned the farmer about how animals were born. The children also inspected growing crops, and listened in wonder to explanations of how farm machinery operated.

When Mrs Thompson showed me the 'farm books' made after the expedition by her class, she still seemed dubious, while I congratulated her on planning and conducting a superb project involving environmental science. At first she was unwilling to accept that nature study and simple biological topics were just as much real science as experiments on magnets, electric currents and tuning forks. So I tried to define for her what primary science was. Since I believe that a syllabus of specific facts and principles belongs to secondary education, I attempted to give a description of the *process* of science in action.

The temperamental spur to scientific activity is curiosity.

Toddlers share this tendency with other animals. When my teenage son erected a tent on the lawn, a neighbour's cat that was always alert and ready to play inspected the outside and inside of the alien contraption, before proceeding on its way. Thus, too, little children respond to novelty – if we let them . . . They explore with all their senses. Unfortunately babies put objects into their mouths, and must be stopped. At school, infants concentrate on using the senses of sight, touch and hearing. Infants stroking and manipulating the bones of a skeleton were 'seeing' its structure by touch, as well as by sight.

Children at a country infant school were fortunate in having several teachers interested in ornithology. Surrounded by fields, the school was ideally situated for observing nature. Many children learned to identify a great variety of birds, by song as well as by sight. Records were kept of the number of sightings for different species – and of the number of days different birds could be heard singing. All the children were encouraged to keep 'bird books' containing original impressions of birds' appearances. *The scientific activity of deliberate observation acted as raw material for both mathematical and verbal communication for these children.*

Students and teachers complain that children do not ask many questions. Despite this, modern primary science teaching methods depend heavily on 'child-centredness' – an implicit assumption that children will put what puzzles them into words, and thereby generate their own investigations. This utopian idea is probably derived from the fact that mature adult scientists make questioning a key practice of their procedure. Children do ask questions. During a lesson in which the teacher featured the human skeleton, an infant wanted to know what a cat's bones were like. But the teacher, keeping to her already plotted course, postponed an answer – and, later, forgot . . .

Children do ask questions – and we notice them, if we really listen. The trouble is that, traditionally, education is largely a communicative process, for passing on a body of knowledge, and for preserving national culture and social organisation. The examination system deifies memory. With so much to impart, and too little time, teachers feel pressed to cram knowledge into minds. Far better – amidst an avalanche of new knowledge, more overwhelming day by day – to encourage children to think. A questioning, critical attitude helps an individual to know what he needs to know, and to reject the rest. That is why I think that to encourage children's questions is so important.

Certain types of questions can be answered by observation and experiment. What is the difference between common frogs and toads? In the absence of actual specimens, good pictures can be provided for children to compare. But there is no substitute for actually feeling the cold slippery exterior of a nervous frog, or lightly grasping a plump 'warty'-skinned toad.

If a teacher can relax and honestly share children's ignorance, to join them in seeking answers to questions, and if a teacher can show genuine pleasure when the answers are found, that teacher will be setting an excellent example of the scientific attitude.

An infants' teacher let her children draw around their hands on to newspaper, after which the 'hands' were cut out and pasted on to black paper. Then each child grabbed a handful of beans from a bowl. Beans were counted, and the totals written next to appropriate cutouts on the 'chart'. Did the biggest hand grab the most beans? Actually, John, with the stubbiest fingers, was 'winner' – but his palm was broad. Was it long fingers, or a broad palm (or some other factor) which made for better bean-grasping? *These children were appreciating that several variable influences might affect the result of an operation. Science and mathematics were taking root here.*

Showing curiosity, observing, communicating, asking questions, comparing, seeking answers to questions through observation and experiment (doing a 'fair test'), appreciating variables, and basing conclusions upon evidence: these actions typify a process approach to science. To be a science educator, a teacher needs more common sense than bookish background knowledge (the knowledge comes with experience), but above all a teacher must have confidence – and good class control. Heedless of a syllabus, mindful of obligations to extend children's basic communication, number and physical skills, a primary teacher can – if so desiring – be a science educator every day.

Worrying about 'right' answers

If I don't know much science myself, how do I know whether the result of a child's experiment is correct?

Many teachers of infants and juniors worry about this. Scientific facts exploited by technology are often very difficult. Even 'elementary' principles can be hard to grasp, without a great deal of first-hand experience and thought. But, besides knowledge, there is another side to science. Indeed, knowledge and its applications are only the end products of a most effective problem-solving *process*.

The process begins with observing and giving names, and proceeds with the recognition of questions. A clearly stated question is itself a fine achievement, because it can suggest an answer. For example, a child is taught that a certain red-painted horsehoe-shaped object that attracts nails is called a magnet. The child soon notices that the magnet apparently picks up only metal objects. A wise teacher will ask the child if the magnet attracts all metals. (It is better if the child asks the question, but not essential.) Then the child is encouraged to carry out many tests.

This is where the trouble begins. For a start, the child has to be taught the names of some common metals. That will be useful anway. However, many metal objects, such as cans and drawing pins, are plated with other metals. A treacle 'tin' is 98 per cent iron, plated with tin and partly covered with printer's ink. And a steel drawing pin might be coated to look like brass. It is well known that (*a*) a metal can or pin are coated, and (*b*) the coating metals themselves are not attracted to magnets. How can we stop the child from learning that tin and brass are magnetic?

The trouble is worse if the non-specialist teacher also is unaware of these anomalies. *Perhaps the biggest obstacle to making 'correct' observations is the feeling on the part of the teacher that conclusions need to be final.* In science nothing is final. The truth is always subverted by deeper truth. Once atoms were thought of as tiny indestructible solid balls. Then they appeared to be like miniature solar systems, consisting mainly of space. Now we must try to imagine the particles in those 'solar systems' as being also like waves of energy.

It might be useful advice to keep statements about scientific observations as honest as possible. If a magnet attracts what appears to be a brass (really brass-coated) drawing pin, don't generalise by saying that the magnet attracts brass. It is more truthful to report that the magnet attracts a 'brass' drawing pin. Later, when it is seen that a brass door knocker does not stick to the magnet, the question arises: Why does a magnet attract one 'brass' object and not another? The way is now left open for a more profound discovery. Sooner or later, when the child learns about metal plating, it will be possible for the child to understand that brass never was attracted to the magnet. The pin was attracted because it was mostly made of iron.

It may be thought that the example given is a long-winded way to learn a few facts. That would be true if facts alone were important. There is, however, no consensus of knowledge that can be regarded as a primary science syllabus. That belongs to the secondary school. But cautious practice of the scientific process is of inestimable value in educating children to think, to base opinions on evidence, and to come to terms with scientific concepts (for example, force, germination and solubility) through the manipulation of materials. Books can supply wanted names, suggest new topics and techniques – and help in confirming first-hand impressions.

But teachers feel safest when they can keep children's learning within the sphere of their own expertise, so it may be advisable to steer children's questioning towards investigations already familiar to the teacher. Such a course does not compromise the process method: it merely limits the originality of the work. There is nothing wrong with children beating new paths to old discoveries. Children's work is always original – in the sense of being realised and expressed for the first time – if we let them get on with it themselves. It is important that children feel something of the enthusiasm and excitement of questing scientists.

When science is taught this way, integrity of approach is paramount, and results are judged 'correct' in so far as the process is rigorously followed. It will not always be possible to check results with 'official' answers in books. Therefore young scientists should be urged to question the validity of their findings. (Did the experiments take all known factors into account? Were the tests done carefully enough, and a sufficient number of times?) Ironically, it may be healthy for children to learn to doubt a little. Then there will always be room in their minds for modification of their knowledge, and change.

2
Using Key Concepts as Guidelines for Children Aged Five to Ten

I understand if:
1   *I can state it in my own words . . .*
2   *I can give examples of it . . .*
3   *I can recognise it in different forms . . .*
4   *I can see connections with other ideas . . .*
5   *I can make use of it in various ways . . .*
6   *I can foresee some of its consequences . . .*
7   *I can state its opposite . . .*

Science in the primary school means 'Developing an enquiring mind and a scientific approach to problems' (*Science 5/13*). This definition puts emphasis on pupil activity and a special way of thinking – what I have called 'being a simple scientist'. To be a scientist you have to perform certain skills. They include observing (with all the senses), measuring, comparing, sorting, describing, recording numerical data, identifying variables, predicting, and experimenting (doing fair tests). I should also mention questioning.

'That is all very well,' say teachers. 'But what do we actually teach the children?' To which I reply, 'Most subject-matter in the primary school can be studied in a scientific way.' The teachers are often not satisfied with this, so I say that the compendious Teacher's Guides associated with the *Science 5/13* project contain many times more ideas than any teacher will ever need to teach science effectively. But the sheer volume of the *Science 5/13* material proves too daunting for the average primary school teacher.

The teachers sincerely ask for more specific guidelines. So how can teachers be helped to penetrate the luxuriant jungle of ideas which *Science 5/13* might be said to resemble? An answer could be to make a list of the sorts of concepts that children can be expected to learn from their work in science. Dr Wynne Harlen, the evaluator for the *Science 5/13* project, has done just that in an article titled 'Does Content Matter in Primary Science?' (*The School Science Review*, June 1978).

I have attempted to beat a path through the 'jungle', going between a commitment to a so-called skills-based (process) teaching method, and the concepts suggested by Wynne Harlen. My 'path' consists of ideas for lesson content – not all of which are to be found in *Science 5/13*. My hope is that teachers will find some of the ideas a source of inspiration when putting together their own science teaching programmes and schemes.

Concepts about ourselves and other living things

Living things have the capability of reproducing themselves, and this takes place in different ways in different plants and animals, but for each the pattern is the same in each generation.

Living things grow and develop, and this requires food.

Human beings must have certain kinds of food for growth, energy, and to fight disease.

Human beings gain information about their surroundings through their senses. There are limits to the range and sensitivity of the sense organs, but these can be increased by using tools, or instruments.

Ideas for lesson content

1 Pick some seeds off a dandelion clock. Try to grow dandelions from them. Let any new flowers go to seed.

2 Collect seeds (everything from radish to horse chestnut). Talk about where they come from. Plant some and see how they grow.

3 Discover seeds inside 'juicy fruits' (apple, orange, blackberry, haw). Base well-observed art and written work on the discoveries.

4 Examine unshelled peanuts. Where do they come from? Break them open. Are 'peanuts' seeds? Plant some. (Soak in water overnight first.)

5 Breeding rabbits, gerbils, or guinea-pigs will provide natural occasions for talking about reproduction in mammals.

6 Find some toads or frogs spawning, and try to observe the growth cycle from egg to toadlet or froglet.

7 Look for butterflies' eggs (on cabbage), or caterpillars. Set. up a 'butterfly cage' in which to observe metamorphosis.

8 Record the numbers of seeds found inside fruits picked from the same plant. Will all the seeds germinate on damp blotting paper?

9 Look for patterns in the structures and arrangements of flowers and leaves. How are the species similar, or different?

10 Study books that give clear pictures of the stages of animals' life histories. *But also try to observe the actual animals.*

11 Some animals change more dramatically than others as they develop (frog, butterfly). Can we have a 'baby butterfly'?

12 Dissect embryos from wet broad bean seeds. Will they grow on damp blotting paper? What if we 'feed' them with sugared water?

13 Visit a farm. Ask the farmer questions about how he feeds his animals, and about how quickly the pigs, sheep and hens grow into adults.

14 Can the school dinners supervisor come to talk with the children about the importance of different foodstuffs for their health?

15 Do grown-ups resemble themselves as babies? Examine photographs loaned by parents. Talk about changes associated with 'growing up'.

16 With a paper cylinder over the head and shoulders, attempt to identify mystery objects by touch.

17 Make 'feely pictures' by sticking interestingly-textured objects and material on to cards. With eyes closed, appreciate them by touch.

18 Listen to a heart beating, using a big plastic funnel as a 'stethoscope'. Does the beat sound faster after vigorous exercise?

19 A magnifying glass may be said to make the eye 'more powerful'. Use plastic magnifying glasses to make discoveries.

20 Spend some time listening for and identifying sounds indoors. Go out on a 'listening walk'. Devise a quiz of sounds.

21 Prepare a 'smelly quiz' with substances placed inside covered yogurt pots. Who, when blindfolded, can identify the most smells?

22 How close to a page must the reader be, to read the words on it? Is it the same distance for everybody? Make a graph of the distances.

23 Talk about 'My Favourite Taste'. Try to describe tastes. Try tasting small pieces of fruits, whilst pinching the nostrils.

24 What inventions make things look (*a*) bigger? (*b*) closer? Enjoy experiences with a *low-power* microscope, and with binoculars.

25 Use wooden rollers (cut from broom handles) to move a heavy concrete slab. Experiment with levers. (Safety!)

Concepts about forces, movement and energy

To make anything move (or change the direction in which it is moving) there has to be something pushing, pulling, or twisting it.

When a push or a pull makes something move it requires energy which can come from various sources: food, fuel, electricity, a wound spring, etc.

All things are pulled down towards the earth. The amount of this pull is the weight of the object.

The speed of an object means how far it moves in a certain time.

Ideas for lesson content

1 Young children can appreciate 'forces' as pushes and pulls and twisting, felt during work and play. Always use the appropriate words.

2 People, bulldozers, tractors, diesel engines and magnets can push and pull. Cranes pull up loads. Explosions push with great force.

3 Collect 'working' toys that are driven by pulling (magnetic fishing), pushing (pop gun), and twisting ('helicopter' top).

4 During a project on 'Transport' discuss the ways driving forces act. Wind pushes a sail. Engines pull trains. A motor turns a propeller.

5 Draw some of the ways in which things can be made to move by pulling (on a rope), pushing (kicking a ball), or twisting (turning a key).

6 Go on a class visit to a playground or fair ground. Find examples of pulling, pushing and twisting forces. Talk about them.

7 Can we think of motion happening without forces acting? Clouds? What about the loud bang that makes our windows shake?

8 Is energy needed to make sounds? Try to find examples of sounds produced without movement somewhere or other. Talk about this.

9 Put confetti into a balloon. Inflate it. How have we stored energy in the balloon? Pop it. An explosion forces confetti everywhere.

10 How does a mousetrap work? (Safety!) We say that the spring can store energy. What does this mean? A demonstration . . .

11 Fly a cheap, rubber band powered toy aeroplane. Talk about how the twisted rubber is able to store and then release energy to drive the plane.

12 Chemicals 'act on each other' inside a battery, producing electric current. Study how the electricity makes light and motion in torches and toys.

13 Stir a teaspoonful of Andrews' Liver Salts into a half glassful of water. Where does the energy in the 'fizz' come from?

14 The *force* of gravity is the pull of the earth that makes things fall and feel heavy. Talk about falling things, 'heavy' and 'light' things . . .

15 When children are playing on a see-saw, talk about how their weights 'make the forces' which cause the see-saw to go up and down.

16 Weigh ten common objects. Make a picture chart showing 'How much gravity can pull on these things' (in order, from least to most).

17 Hang an iron nut on a rubber band. Weight forces the rubber to stretch. Use a magnet to make it seem as if the nut gets heavier.

18 Feel, and talk about why, a house-brick under water seems lighter. Why can a hippopotamus move about so gracefully under water?

19 How does a parachute make an object fall to the earth more slowly? Talk about how the 'force of air resistance' opposes gravity.

20 The moon's gravitational pull is only one-sixth of earth's gravity. So how much would a teacher or child weigh on the moon?

21 Measure 50 metres. Hold a race. Children will take different times to run the same distance. Talk about this.

22 Look up the top speeds of various animals. With the children, make a graph to show how far these animals *might* run in one hour.

23 Take two identical sheets of paper. Roll one into a tight ball. Drop both together from the same height. Which falls faster?

24 Have a woodlouse race. Starting from a central spot on a large paper, measure how far each creature can travel in one minute.

25 Hold a snail race. Use a stop clock, chalk and string to compare how far several wet snails travel in five minutes. Which snail is 'Speedy'?

Concepts about the physical surroundings

Patterns occur in weather conditions and cycles in the apparent movement of the sun and moon and in changes in plants in the immediate environment.

The materials described as stone, wood, glass, plastic, metal have certain sets of properties which help to identify them.

There are definite differences in the way matter behaves when it is solid, liquid or gaseous.

Some substances dissolve in water very well, others only a little and some not at all.

Some substances float in water, others sink. Substances which sink can be used to make things which float.

Ideas for lesson content

1 Keep a weather chart. Record wind direction. Collect rainfall in a wide tin, and display daily yields (ink-stained) in narrow tubes.

2 Talk about day length, temperature, and weather characteristic of the seasons. Can the children remember last year's seasons?

3 Point to the sun. (Safety!) Was it roughly in the same part of the sky this time ('dinner time') yesterday? Will it be in the same part at the same time tomorrow?

4 In winter, when children are most likely to notice the moon, ask them to draw the moon's current appearance. Talk about the 'phases'.

5 Study the changes during the year in a tree near the school. Were they similar last year? Will they be the same next year?

6 Collect and identify some metals. How are they alike, or different? Test them with a magnet. Do they conduct electricity?

7 Assemble a good assortment of stones and pebbles. Let the children invent reasons for sorting them in different ways.

8 Exhibit everyday objects made with plastic and glass. Talk about their contrasting and similar properties. Discuss their advantages and disadvantages.

9 Is all wood alike? What are the differences? Find some hard and soft woods. List uses, including for fuel and paper-making.

10 What materials are used in building the school? How are their special properties exploited? Could we build and live in a paper house?

11 Trap a sample of air in a plastic bag. (Safety!) Close the bag by twisting. Think of five ways to describe the gas inside.

12 Notice how bonfire smoke steals, like a blue mist, through a wood. Observe chimney smoke rising vertically on a still and frosty morning.

13 Watch a kettle boiling. (Safety!) What is happening to the water? What happens when you put some of the water in a freezer?

14 Tip a bucket of water near the top end of a gently sloping, uneven playground. Put chalk marks where it flows. Talk about this.

15 Create little puddles on the playground one sunny afternoon. Chalk around their edges each ¼ hour, as they dry up. Talk about this.

16 Talk about what is seen to happen when a sugar lump is put into water. Wait, then stir the water. Where does the dissolving sugar go to?

17 How many sugar lumps can be dissolved in a jar of cold water? Does the sugar dissolve (*a*) more, (*b*) quicker, in very warm water?

18 Is there anything dissolved in rain water? Let rain fall on to clean glass. Let it dry. Where did the dissolved stuff come from?

19 Set up a 'Dissolving Lab' on a table. Test common, named substances. Record results as 'very', 'slightly', or 'not' soluble.

20 Young children will confuse dissolving with melting. Let a wax candle melt and drip into cold water. What happens? Does it dissolve?

21 Create a 'Floating and Sinking Lab'. Test common objects. Record sets of 'floaters' and 'sinkers'. What about a glass jar?

22 When children have found by practice that Plasticine sinks, ask them to find a way to make it float. *Do not actually mention boats!*

23 Load a polystyrene tile with coins or washers, until it sinks. Use plastic bags, or ping-pong balls, to make a 'sinker' float.

24 An aluminium foil cake case floats. Fold it into a pellet. Flatten it with a hammer. Does the 'solid' aluminium float?

25 Buy a cheap toy 'diver', or submarine (operated by blowing and sucking through a tube). Play with it, and talk about how it works.

Basic concepts

The length of an object remains the same when only its position is changed, even though it may look different.

The area is the amount of surface across the face of an object. It is unaffected by moving or dividing up the surface.

The capacity of a container is the amount of space within it which can be filled. The volume of an object is the amount of space it takes up.

A quantity of matter which exists at a certain time will still exist at a later time, either in the same form or in other forms.

Objects or events can be classified in several ways, according to their features or characteristics.

Certain actions always have the same consequences, and this relationship can often be used to predict the effect of changes.

Ideas for lesson content

1 Observe how the shadows of familiar objects change (broom, umbrella, teddy bear) when they are held different ways in the sunlight.

2 Stand upon a certain spot at half-hourly intervals through a sunny day. Let a friend chalk around the shadow. The shadow changes. Do you?

3 Does a friend really get smaller whilst running away into the distance? (Would it really be possible to put him into a matchbox?)

4 Appearances of people change when they are looked directly down on from above. Draw how they look. Do they really change?

5 Copy impressions of a toy car viewed from different angles. The drawings will look different. But does the car really change?

6 Talk about how we know that people in the distance are not in fact as small as they might appear. Estimate the heights of distant things.

7 Let the children make Tangram pictures from identical gummed paper sets. Talk about who would have most, if the shapes were made of toffee.

8 Compare areas, by drawing around hands or leaves, on small-squared paper. Who would have most, if the pictures were made of gold?

9 Let each child draw an object by colouring in only ten squares on graph paper. Who would have most, if the pictures were made of gold?

10 How do we find the area of a cube's surface? Do all of its six faces cover the same number of little squares?

11 Compare the capacities of an assortment of containers, by carefully counting in cupfuls of water. Do different children get similar results?

12 If volume is defined as the amount of space an object takes up, we should be able to compare volumes by immersing objects in a jar of water.

13 Young children will probably find the concept of displacement difficult. *Listen* to their comments on the idea. Compare fist sizes by displacement.

14 Seal a large ice cube inside a plastic bag. Let the ice melt. Will the water weigh more or less than the ice?

15 As time passes, mothballs shrink. What happens to them? Are they slowly vanishing? What about the mothball smell?

16 Arrange a collection of toy cars in various ways. Does it sometimes *look* as if there are more cars? Talk about this. Count the cars.

17 When water is spilt on the floor, why does it spread out so much? Does the quantity increase? Experiment to find out.

18 Obtain a cheap but large mixture of foreign stamps from a dealer. Let the children sort them out, according to several criteria.

19 Make a collection of 'Happy Colours' and 'Sad Colours'. Do some children disagree about the classifications?

20 Identify five birds that live in woods, five that visit gardens, and five that are found near water. Might any appear in more than one set?

21 Identify ten animals that crawl along the ground, ten that can run, and ten that can swim. Might any appear in more than one set?

22 What will happen if we switch off the classroom heating? How can we keep warm, without the heating on? What would happen if the sun 'went out'?

23 Put seeds to germinate indoors (*a*) with water, (*b*) without water. What happens? Why must we water the garden during a drought?

24 When the moon looks like the letter C (or the letter D), will it look bigger, or smaller, the next night?

25 What happens when we leave bare iron objects outdoors? Talk about possible reasons for rusting. How can we prevent iron things rusting?

3
Using Key Concepts as Guidelines for Children Aged Eleven and Twelve

Teachers who feel intimidated by process approaches to primary science education may welcome guidelines listing concepts which children may acquire before leaving the primary school. My metaphor is 'concept targets'. The idea is attractive because it can provide a consensus of cognitive aims, whilst freeing teachers to approach the concepts by ways and means uniquely their own. I have already responded to a list of such concepts, compiled by Wynne Harlen. These covered the age range between five and ten years. I have suggested ideas, as *examples* of lesson material that might be used to help primary school children to reach the concept targets. I wanted to provide teachers with starting-points for thinking out their own, more relevant ideas. Also, I wanted to help teachers to recognise the sorts of opportunities which can arise spontaneously, from everyday work, for teaching particular concepts. The suggestions that follow cover the remainder of Dr Harlen's list, for children up to the ages of eleven and twelve. As before, I have avoided ideas calling for a lot of equipment, especially expensive items.

About ourselves and other living things

The basic life processes are growth, feeding, respiration, excretion, reproduction, sensitivity to the surroundings, and some mechanism for movement and support.

There is a great variety in the way in which these life processes are carried out by different living things.

In the human body organs are grouped into systems, each concerned with one of the main processes.

Energy is needed by all living things to support life processes.

Animals take in food, plants use the sun's energy to produce food they can use and store. Living things depend on each other for their survival and all animals depend ultimately on plants for their food.

Living things have changed very gradually through time by a process of adaptation to various external conditions. The most successful animals at any time are those best suited to the present conditions.

Ideas for lesson content

1 Make a list of things that grow, but which are not alive (a snowball rolling downhill, a cloud, a balloon being inflated, a shadow, this list).

2 A mechanical duck can move, quack, swallow bread pellets, and excrete a whitish substance. Does this mean that the duck is alive?

3 Record the 'weight' gained by a baby gerbil, day by day. Is this the same as the weight of food and drink consumed by the animal?

4 Observe a toad breathing. Find an insect's breathing holes (using a low-power binocular microscope). Find a snail's breathing hole.

5 A goldfish keeps gulping water. Where does this water go to? What is the goldfish doing? Dissect the gills of a herring.

6 Observe a newt. How does it walk? How does it swim? How does it eat a small earthworm? Investigate how long a newt can remain underwater.

7 Study a series of clear, sensitively drawn diagrams about human reproduction. Discuss how babies are conceived, born, and cared for.

8 Draw around a lettuce leaf on to squared paper, to discover how much a snail can eat in five minutes. (Starve the snail for 2 days first.)

9 Imagine being made of jelly! Or possessing a rigid skeleton! Examine a skeleton. Appreciate having muscles and articulated bones.

10 How many ways can the children sense changes in their surroundings? (Also consider a 'sense of body posture', or a 'time sense', etc.)

11 Can a rattlesnake 'see' in the dark? It has an organ which is sensitive to infra-red (heat) rays emitted by small desert animals.

12 Scientists have found minute quantities of a magnetic substance inside the heads of carrier pigeons. How might pigeons find their way home?

13 Giant Japanese catfish get nervous some time before an earthquake. Find out more examples of animals (and plants) which have 'super' senses.

14 Let the children draw and label their impressions of what the insides of their bodies *might* be like. Compare results with a 'take-apart' model.

15 Use the anatomical model (from a secondary school) to identify interrelated systems devoted to respiration, circulation, excretion, etc.

16 After a discussion, let the children chart 'feeding-chains', showing how living things need to feed on other living things.

17 Actual food chains inevitably begin with plants. How do plants 'feed'? Heed and evaluate the children's original ideas.

18 What happens when cress seeds grown in the dark are compared with similar ones grown in the light? What might the light be supplying?

19 How long would a hawk survive if, suddenly, there were no green plants anywhere? (Hawks feed on small herbivorous animals.)

20 Where did the energy in coal and oil come from? Why are these substances called 'fossil fuels'? Why is our dependence on them unwise?

21 Ancient solar energy is 'stored' in coal. What do the children think this idea means? *It is always important to evaluate their ideas.*

22 Imagine the sun ceasing to exist. What would happen to life on earth? Let the children write down their own ideas *before* the discussion begins.

23 Study the 'evolution' of flying machines from balloons to spacecraft. What evidence is there that living things have evolved in some natural way?

24 How do we know that giant dinosaurs ever existed? Why do the children think they died out? (Are birds warm-blooded 'dinosaurs'?)

25 How do human beings survive in alien environments (the Arctic, desert, undersea, the moon)? What are the advantages? What are the dangers?

About forces, movement and energy

A force is needed to accelerate or decelerate a thing which is moving, or to change the direction of its movement.

When an object is not moving (or moving at a constant speed) the forces acting on it are equal and opposite.

All things which are moving have energy and when they slow down some of their energy is changed into another form.

Friction is a force which commonly opposes motion.

Energy is changed from one form to another in a variety of processes. It is never lost, but what disappears in one form reappears in another.

Ideas for lesson content

1 Talk about how a motor car is forced to start, to stop, to change speed, to alter its direction of motion. Where do the different forces act?

2 Study the ways forces are made to act on rudders and other 'control surfaces', to change the direction of motion of ships and aeroplanes.

3 Does the motion of an object ever change, without another force acting? Think deeply about this. What forces slow down and stop a rolling ball?

4 A force can change the shape of an object. How does motion take place in such cases? (Think about the flowing of moulded clay, stretching rubber.)

5 Fix magnets to little model railway trucks. Use the pull of attraction and the push of repulsion to make the 'trains' move.

6 The earth is like a huge magnet that acts on a compass. The magnetism is invisible. Use a pair of magnets to explore 'invisible forces'.

7 When a magnetic compass-needle twists around on its pivot to point N and S, what is the force (or forces) acting on its ends?

8 Magnetic attraction and repulsion are 'action-at-a-distance-forces'. Are there others besides magnetism? (Electrostatic forces, gravitation.)

9 Use a balloon rubbed with wool to explore electrostatic attraction. How can two such balloons be used to demonstrate electrostatic repulsion?

10 Is electrostatic force the same as magnetism? Will a magnet attract little pieces of paper? Will a magnet repel a rubber balloon?

11 Gravitation is an at-a-distance-force. How do we measure the pull of gravity on objects? We weigh them. Weight is a force – a pull.

12 If all things are pulled down towards the earth by gravity (the special name for earth's gravitation), what about rising balloons?

13 Does gravity pull down on a floating ship? Yes. But the sea pushes up on the ship (and the 'ocean of air' supports a balloon) against gravity.

14 Can we go by balloon to the moon? Why not? Could we go up in a balloon from the surface of the moon? (The moon has no atmosphere.)

15 To compare the weight of potatoes on the earth with their weight on the moon, would it matter if you used either scales or a spring balance?

16 How can we 'put energy into' a rubber band, golf-ball, air-gun, record player, alarm clock, a glider, or the water wheel at the Old Mill?

17 Wind up and put down a clockwork bird or frog. Observe the action. Where does its energy come from? Where was its energy stored?

18 Spin one of those metal toy humming tops, worked by 'pumping' up and down (pulling and pushing) on a handle. How is the sound made?

19 Energy is the 'go' of things . . . What eventually happens to the energy making the top spin? In what ways does friction force the top to stop?

20 Press your hands together hard, whilst rubbing vigorously. How do they feel? Hot! Motion energy is being converted into heat energy.

21 Can the children imagine a logical chain of ideas connecting the toy animal (see 17) with the sun? (Sun – energy waves – growing corn – etc.)

22 What sorts of movements are produced from the energy we can set free from petrol, cornflakes, the sun, coal, tight springs, electricity?

23 How does the energy 'stored' in a fuel (such as oil) differ from energy stored in a wound-up spring, or in a mountain lake?

24 Human beings run on 'solar energy'! Explain. What are food calories? Which foods provide us with the most energy?

25 How did energy get up into a mountain lake? How might we use the energy from the lake? (We could build a power station.)

About the physical surroundings

Air fills the space around us and contains oxygen, which living things need.

Air contains water vapour, some of which condenses out in various conditions to give rain, dew, mist, snow, hail, ice or water.

Soil is composed of small fragments from rocks, air, water and decayed remains from living materials which provide substances needed by growing plants. These substances have to be replenished to keep soil fertile.

All non-living things are made from substances found in the earth. Their supply is not endless, so they must not be wasted.

Pollution of the air, water, or land by waste, smoke, or noise can harm both living and non-living things.

The earth is one of nine planets so far known to be circling the sun, which is our source of heat and light energy.

The moon circles the earth, reflecting light from the sun.

Melting or evaporating requires energy in the form of heat.

A complete circuit of conducting material is needed for electricity to flow.

Ideas for lesson content

1 Suck out the air from a plastic detergent bottle. What causes the bottle to collapse? (Might something be pressing on the outside?)

2 Wedge a damp blotting paper package, containing iron filings, in the bottom of a glass tube. Invert the tube in a jar filled with water.

3 Set up several such tubes, to investigate the proportion of oxygen in the air (Rusting uses up oxygen. Water rises to fill the space.)

4 Would it be less cruel to keep a goldfish in a bowl if the bowl were equipped with an aerating device?

5 Why must an astronaut wear a spacesuit on the moon? Why are there (at present) no plants on the moon? Do any plants grow in deserts?

6 Where might water go to when it evaporates? Test 'evaporation rate' using equal amounts of water put into vessels of differing diameters.

7 Water 'goes into the air'. Can we get it back again? What is a cloud? (A parachutist falling through a cloud gets wet . . .)

8 After a cloudless night, examine dewdrops on a spider's web. And why is the grass wet? Where did the water come from?

9 What is the 'smoke' seen in breath on freezing mornings? What happens to clothing when people go out in a heavy mist?

10 What makes 'weather', other than the presence of water in the air? Study the weather forecasts in the *local* newspaper. Are they accurate?

11 Try to grow a mature plant from a bean, by putting it next to wet blotting paper in a jar. Why does it begin growing well before failing?

12 Let each child mix a teacupful of soil in a large jar of water. Solid matter should settle overnight. Talk about what happens.

13 Decomposed bodies of dead plants and animals supply 'chemicals' vital to keep living things alive. What if dead things never decayed?

14 Seal *slightly* moistened bread inside a plastic bag. Wait a few days. Talk about any moulds that grow. (Throw away the bag unopened.)

15 Why do farmers and gardeners use fertilisers, compost and manure? Grow grass samples, with and without appropriate amounts of fertilisers.

16 The earth is a spaceship . . . Will the earth's mineral and fuel reserves last for ever? Discuss the wisest ways to run Spaceship Earth.

17 If the world's population is continually increasing, how can we hope to feed, and to provide a comfortable life for everybody in the future?

18 From data in an astronomy book, construct a model to show the relative sizes of planets, and their relative distances from the sun.

19 Survey the litter on the school campus. Collect and classify. Map the 'litter spots'. Take action to keep the area tidier.

20 Visit the local pond, stream, or river. Are there any obvious signs of pollution? What sorts of animals and plants are found there?

21 What do *you* feel about excessive noise? Do the children know any cases of noise being harmful? How do we educate people to live quietly?

22 How do buildings in cities get black and grimy? Do old buildings in the country look so dirty? (Lichens are a sign of clean air . . .)

23 Experiment with a tennis ball 'earth', a ping pong ball 'moon', and a 60W lamp 'sun', in a dark room. What makes the moon shine?

24 Heat is an important form of energy. (Does 'heat' cost money?) Heat melts butter and tar. Heat dries the washing. Talk about drought.

25 Construct a model lighthouse with a flashing light. Or a robot figure with flashing eyes. (Buy 'flasher' bulbs at an automobile supplies shop.)

Basic concepts

The total volume of an object is not changed by dividing it up or changing its shape.

The process of measurement is the repeated comparison of a quantity with an agreed unit of the quantity. All measurements, however careful or fine, are inexact to some degree.

All changes in objects or substances are caused by interaction with other substances or by adding or taking away energy.

Ideas for lesson content

1 Talk with the children about how the clever commercial packaging of products can confuse us into expecting more for our money than we get.

2 How much space inside a chocolate box actually contains chocolate? (Model the chocolates in plasticine, before beating them into a cube.)

3 In a box of cornflakes, how much space is occupied by the product? (To be fair, the flakes do pack more tightly during transit . . .)

4 How much does a child weigh? How accurate can the answer be? (Investigate what factors make the body weight vary all the time.)

5 Compare and talk about block graphs made from data obtained by weighing classes of first and fourth year juniors.

6 The normal human pulse rate is often said to be 72 beats per second. Compare the children's pulses. Do heart beats and pulses coincide?

7 Chart top speeds of various animals. (Look in the *Guinness Book of Records*.) How reliable are the facts? Can facts be useful if they are uncertain?

8 What is the size of an oak tree's leaves? Pick 50 from the same tree. Measure them. How can a meaningful answer be given?

9 How can a page from a telephone directory be weighed on bathroom scales? Assume that all the pages have equal weights.

10 Test the powers of magnets by finding out through how many playing cards they will attract a pin. Are both ends of a magnet equally strong?

11 Stand a child of known height at the bottom of a tree. Judge how many of these 'child units' equal the height of the tree.

12 Use a method based on the proportional relationship between height and shadow length to find the height of the same tree.

13 Discuss the reliability of the above methods. Would anyone be interested in a much more exact measurement? Invent a better way.

14 Stretch a rubber band to ten times its original length. How does it feel when held against the lips? Let it contract. Test it again.

15 What evidence is there for thinking that water uses up energy when it evaporates? (Feel what happens whilst meths evaporates from the skin.)

16 When iron rusts it takes something from the air. (Oxygen.) In what ways can we prevent this unwelcome change from happening?

17 Write a 'secret' message, using a clean pen dipped in lemon juice. The invisible writing changes, becoming visible, when the paper is warmed.

18 'Thawpit' (carbon tetrachloride) dissolves and removes greasy marks. Find out how other sorts of stains can be removed.

19 Blow through a straw into limewater (from a secondary school). Something in the breath causes a dramatic change. Consult a textbook.

20 Heat is a form of energy. Study the changes in the state of water which produce weather. Is the energy being added, or taken away?

21 Find out from books how steam-engines work. Trace the history of steam-engines during the eighteenth and nineteenth centuries.

22 Play with a 'friction drive' toy car which has its top removed. See how the flywheel in the motor stores energy and releases it again.

23 Motion always means that energy is being expended. How do we give a glider the energy it needs to fly? How is this energy lost again?

24 Everyone is talking about the Energy Crisis. Why is the world's immense dependence on 'fossil fuels' a major cause of worry?

25 The earth's spinning on its axis causes day and night. Day and night are consequences of the supply or denial of solar energy . . .

4
Science with Infants

Smashing bubbles and vanishing sugar

Anyone can blow bubbles through a plastic drinking straw, one end of which has been slit several times lengthways, allowing thin strips of the side to be bent outward, forming a terminal flower-like structure five centimetres in diameter. Very young children need help with making these cheap 'bubble pipes', but they soon learn to use them – after dipping the prepared end into a yogurt pot containing a strong solution of liquid detergent in water. The quantity should be small, in case the children spill it over the tables. If the wetted pipe is pointed downward, very gentle blowing through the untreated end should produce a growing bubble. A teacher is advised to master the art, before working with children. Then it will be possible to give expert assistance to those children who inevitably have difficulties.

Bubble-blowing is a game which can be played for its own sake. Six-year-olds working in groups were rewarded by the thrill of accomplishment. Some of the class blew their bubbles with care; their eyes intent and serious with concentration. Other children, hardly stirring, expressed anxiety, as if waiting for the teacher to come and do the learning for them. Working with the whole class of thirty, the teacher found it tiring to keep up the interest of the successful bubble blowers until everybody had acquired tolerable competence. But learning to blow a bubble is like being able to throw a ball where it is supposed to go. Making any skill one's own is a step on the way to personal control over the environment. Pure science has led to useful technologies which can be seen and felt to be understood. The technology in these children's bubble-blowing led to science.

Later, when the teacher was discussing the lesson with all the children around her, she blew a bubble herself, inviting the children to watch for colours to appear. Observing the hues – sometimes for the first time – the children called out the names: 'white', 'green', 'pink', and 'red'. Colours were visible as the teacher's bubble became thinner. A few of the children could appreciate that a swelling bubble *would* get thinner. But there was confusion in the discussion, because thinking was easily misled by seeing the increasing bulk of the bubble as a whole. *Six-year-olds cannot be expected to take account of more than one variable at once*, which is an important criterion for children's activity in science. No explanation of the colours was necessary at this stage, except perhaps to state emphatically that 'colours are produced when the bubble's side gets thinner'.

Asked to find a word for the bubble shape, many children said 'round'. Another child who had noticed the deformation of natural shape during the blowing, said 'sausage-shaped'. One child knew the word 'sphere'. Stimulated and charmed by the children's pleasure and activity, the teacher racked her memory to recall to *herself* why a freely floating bubble was always spherical. It is because the bubble envelope is elastic. Therefore the skin contracts to the smallest possible surface area for the contained (compressed) air. This is a sphere. (That a sphere is in fact the minimal skin form for any volume is obvious if one imagines trying to change the shape of a hollow rubber ball filled with water, without squeezing out any of the liquid.)

Excitement mounted in the library corner when one or two bubbles fell on to the carpet there – and bounced! A possible explanation was that both the bubble (during blowing) and the carpet (by friction with shoes) were charged with static electricity of the same charge sign. Then, since 'like' charges repel each other, the bubble rebounded upon a weak force field of repulsion. Pressed for an explanation, the teacher might have said, 'Sometimes a bubble won't stick to a piece of carpet, so it bounces instead of bursting.' *A clear statement of the obvious is often the best an honest scientist can do.* But the question was not asked. (In the old days of steam-powered lorries, the issuing 'smoke' often charged the vehicles so potently that a driver on dismounting received a painful electric shock.)

Infants' thinking

In another classroom, younger infants were introduced to the concept of dissolving. Working in pairs, they watched a sugar lump disintegrate in a jar of cold water. Asked beforehand what might happen, the common reply was that it would melt. A single child predicted that the sugar would break up into little bits – a notion on the brink of an atomic theory (which the teacher wisely declined to press any further at this time). Finding it hard to persuade the children that 'dissolving' was the correct word for the phenomenon, the teacher thought that 'melting' might be the natural word for the dissolving idea among her pre-six-year-olds. The remaining fragments of sugar vanished when the children stirred the water, using plastic straws that just happened to be handy. Finally, the teacher asked where the children thought the sugar had gone.

Replies were 'gone into the water', 'up the straw', 'gone inside the water', and 'changed into water' – four ideas which include examples of both intuitive and early concrete operational thinking (in Piagetian terms). The replies 'gone into the water' and 'gone inside the water' betrayed some extension of the previous notion of sugar breaking into little bits. These, in the light of the teacher's superior knowledge, were useful ideas, more advanced than the impressions given by the other children. It is well known that young intuitive thinkers say that a dissolving substance enters the stirring spoon. The reply 'up the straw' was a good example of the spoon hypothesis. But just as interesting was the equally magic-ridden notion that the sugar had literally 'changed into water' – a though which the teacher hoped to dispel by having all the children taste the water.

These case studies of infants at work show how practical science and language development can occur side by side. The science consisted of controlled concrete experience, and the language emphasis was on precision, in direct response to the happenings. Some teachers might think that the activities and organisation described are too formal. This reaction would be reasonable; although it should be appreciated that, within the formal arrangements, the children's own thinking was stimulated. Dogmatic teaching was restrained, often with difficulty by the teachers, who were tempted to test how the brighter children might be drawn beyond their insightful responses. Such restraint might also be controversial! Discipline was generally good, but there were exceptions, such as the little boy in grey, wearing pebbly glasses, who wanted always to 'smash' the bubbles!

Dry bones and breath bags

Once, when I was working with a group of twenty six-year-olds, I asked them; 'What might it be like to be made of jelly?' 'We would all be floppy,' replied Joan. 'We're not really made of jelly,' I continued. 'But we have a lot of soft stuff in our bodies.' The children suggested that bodies are made of skin, blood and cells – while appreciating that an all-jelly person would be unable to stand up or walk. I re-emphasised that we were made of soft materials, before asking what enabled a man to stand erect. 'Bones,' I was told. Many children said 'the skelington', so I paused and attempted to improve the pronunciation by having the whole class repeat the word properly.

'Would you like to see a skeleton?' I said. Then I produced a metre-high scale model, from a basket – although there seemed to be little surprise when it appeared. Only five children thought that the skeleton was ugly. Two precocious boys wanted to ask skeleton riddles. 'He reminds me of the Ghost Train,' said Alan. And Angela was put in mind of a monkey. 'Is this a life-size model of a child's skeleton, or a small model of a grown up's bones?' I asked. Adrian remarked, 'A child wouldn't die that quick – unless he were murdered.' It was most gratifying when a bright boy realised that it could not be a child, because the head was proportionally too small.

The children knew the names of some bones, such as ribs, hips, 'elbow bone', knee-cap, and 'arm bone' (the humerus). I encouraged the children to feel certain bones in themselves, which they could at the same time, see on the model. 'What is inside the ribs?' I wanted to know. The children realised that the heart was there, though nobody mentioned lungs. Some boys laughed, because one of them said 'bosoms', and many children were amused by our skeleton's lack of a 'bottom'.

I invited the children to give the skeleton a name. 'Fred' was offered, and generally preferred to 'Boney'. Afterwards, the children drew impressions of their own skeletons – as an X-ray machine would 'see all inside you'. Fred was on display while the class worked. I did not insist that actual bones be copied, but most children used Fred for reference. Some of the drawings were exceedingly well-observed, while a few depicted purely imaginary bone structures.

Just before lesson two, one week later, I was shown an as-yet headless model skeleton, made by some of the children from cotton-reels, toilet-roll centres, cardboard and string. Once again I asked the children what was to be found inside the ribs. Simon said 'food bags', and prompted Angela to suggest 'breath bags'. Allowing a rather excited class to settle, I demonstrated how I wanted the children to hold their chests, whilst they inhaled deeply. This was hugely enjoyed – the room becoming sibilant with twenty simultaneous deep breaths. Every child felt the breath bags swelling.

'What are the breath bags really called?' I asked. 'Lungs,' said John. And Mary explained that there were two lungs 'like balloons being blown up.' But Simon thought that inhaling lungs were 'like tomatoes growing quickly.' Then, out of the blue, Paul wanted to know why we couldn't learn about a squirrel's or an animal's body. I thereupon took the opportunity to inform the children of their kinship with the entire animal kingdom. 'A human being is an animal, like a badger,' summarised Jane.

I later showed the children a 30cm × 40cm × 20cm (deep) plastic box of water, containing a submerged glass sweet-jar on its side, and a flexible tube. 'How can we use this apparatus to see how much air our lungs can hold?' I asked. 'I know,' said Adrian. 'You could turn the bottle the other way up – and put that (tubing) in, and blow in it, until you can't blow any further.' So I stood the jar of water upside-down in the box. When the jar was thus up-ended, it was considerably taller than the box – but atmospheric pressure on the exposed water's surface stopped water inside the jar from falling down.

'I tried that before,' commented Paul – who no doubt recalled a trick learned through playing with water. (At six, knowing *that* it works is knowing how it works.)

Stuart and Mary volunteered to show the class how much air their lungs could hold. To do this, each child breathed in deeply, before blowing air up into the inverted sweet-jar, via the tubing, to displace the water inside with air. But, before the demonstrations, the children did dummy runs, to make certain that they understood the technique. When Stuart finished his actual demonstration, I put a wide rubber band around his jar, to show how far down his breath had forced the water. Then Mary had her turn, using a second sweet-jar. I then stood the marked jars, side by side and still inverted, on the table, whilst discussing the meaning of the experiment with the interested class.

Most of lesson three was spent giving all the children a chance to 'see' their lung capacities. I appointed Adrian as the experimenter. He supervised the children, one by one, and worked the apparatus without difficulty. Each child measured the depth of the trapped air, using a metric ruler, before counting the equivalent number of squares on a big graph. I outlined the 'bar' in colour, before the child signed his name. Meanwhile, unoccupied children made drawings of the apparatus in action. When I later quizzed the children on their comprehension of the graph, there was little doubt that they understood what it meant.

But it would have been much better if I had used jar-sized cut-outs, to be cut short by each child, according to the individual test result. I have since watched students using this modified method successfully with infants – pasting the shapes on to a 'chart' showing the comparative lung capacities more appropriately.

Finally, in lesson four, I let the children listen directly to one another's heart-beats. This was not so successful as the work with Fred the skeleton and the sweet-jar lung capacity demonstrator. The children could find no words more subtle than 'bang-bang' to describe the beating heart, although some children said they thought the beats were faster after the boys and girls had been running about outside.

5
The Clay Boat Project: floa
sinking studies with infan

Floating and sinking

What we call weight is the force of gravity on the matter, or 'atom stuff' in an object. Density is how much a cubic centimetre weighs. A cubic centimetre of iron is denser than a cubic centimetre of cork, because the iron has more matter in it. Density is the key to understanding floating and sinking. An object floats when it can push away its own weight of water. The water pushed away 'tries' to push back. But displaced water can only push back with the force of its own weight. The 'push back force' of the water is called upthrust, because it seems to be acting only upwards. Iron under water feels lighter, because of water's upthrust acting on it; but the iron sinks fast, because the force of its weight is about eight times greater than the upthrust. (So how much much denser is iron than water?)

Kind reader, be patient a little longer . . . Remember the cork. Put into water, the cork settles down through the surface, until it has pushed away its own weight of water. Then it floats with a large proportion of itself out of the water. This is possible because water is much denser than cork. Cork floats when the downward-acting force of its weight is balanced by the upward-acting force of the water's upthrust. Now relax! These ideas about floating and sinking will not be understood by the average child until about the third year of secondary schooling. But an infant's teacher can put the child on the long intellectual highroad which leads, one day, to Archimedes' Principle of buoyancy, by guiding experience with things which float and things which sink.

...beginning

At the start of the lesson, the class of six-to-seven-year-old boys and girls gathered around a low table. I showed the children ten easy-to-identify objects (big iron nail, stone, white polystyrene ball, lump of Plasticine, cork, wooden brick, pine cone, glass marble, rubber stopper, screw-topped glass jar) and a plastic tank filled with luke-warm water – for it was a cold December morning. Our lesson was a discussion about the materials and whether they might float or sink, if 'tested' in the water. The children guessed, before testing; therefore they were encouraged to make a prediction about each object before we tried the experiment of actually putting it into the water.

The children said that the nail was made of metal, so I asked what the metal was, and they said 'steel'; that I agreed was true, because steel is manufactured from iron. The children were puzzled by the chemist's rubber bung. Timothy called it 'a round'. When I bounced it upon the table and asked everybody to listen, most of the children spoke at once, saying 'rubber'. Then Helen suggested; 'It's a thing that makes the door not bang on the wall.' So we talked for a minute about door stops. Many children recognised that the white ball was made of polystyrene, and the name was properly pronounced by some. Mary said 'polysyrene', and I encouraged her to try again, until she said the word correctly. These examples illustrate how the science was exploited as practice in language skills.

I enquired whether the children thought that polystyrene would float very well, or not very well (another invitation to make a prediction). 'Very well,' thought Simon. 'Why do you think that?' 'Because it's very light,' he replied. Now this implied comparing of weights was the beginning of a concept of density. Cynthia thought that rubber would float. (Was this because it was a bottle stopper and shaped like a cork, which everybody knows will float?) I asked the class, 'Who thinks the rubber will float?' There was a scornful chorus of no's. 'Well let's try it, shall we?' I said. 'Perhaps Cynthia would like to do it.' The rubber sank. Then Simon interrupted with: 'The glass jar will sink.' But Edward and Helen thought it would float – 'Because it's got air inside'.

The jar aroused a lot of interest, because – depending on whether we left its lid on or not – it could be made to float or sink. Even without its lid on, but well ballasted with water, the jar floated. But more water put inside made it sink. Without saying so, we were treating the jar like a submarine. By making its overall density (including the glass and enclosed air) more or less than the density of water, we could make it stay at the surface or submerge. But, as expected, the children concentrated attention on the air inside the jar; so, when it floated, they said it was 'because of the air'. Later, the children made a record of our investigation by sorting out a jumbled list of names printed on the blackboard, into 'things which float' and 'things which sink'.

It was fascinating to notice where the children put the jar. Sometimes it appeared in both lists and occasionally it straddled the dividing line. The lesson finished with a discussion about how the children thought a real submarine worked. Peter said that a submarine went down, 'because it's got weights on, which it drops when it wants to come up'. 'But where,' I asked, 'does it get more weights when it wants to go down?' 'It keeps them on the foredeck,' replied Peter. Jane remarked that a submarine goes down 'because its propellers tip up and drive it down', and Timothy thought that 'it lets some air out'. Molly was intrigued by the submarine's 'little pole', and she informed us, 'Every year a submarine comes with more goods for Oban, in Scotland.'

Now, where do we go from here? For several years before the lesson, the children had opportunities for water play. Perhaps, in future, the class teacher would discuss buoyancy in terms of whether the object in question might have more or less 'heavy stuff'. The term will do for 'matter' in the early years. But the children need to appreciate both the variables, weight and volume, before even a rudimentary awareness of density (how much heavy stuff is packed into a standard cube) is possible at age twelve plus. Though, when I asked the infants: 'Why do you think the wooden block floats deeper than the polystyrene ball?', a child answered 'because the wood is heavier'. And another child said, 'because the wood is smaller'. The answers suggested to me that each child had grasped the importance of one of the variables.

Plasticine boats

During the Second World War, sea-going vessels were moulded from concrete. If this sounds highly unlikely, what about iron steamships? Victorians laughed when daring engineers planned to construct metal boats. Everybody knew from experience that wood (being less dense than water) floated, and that iron (denser than water) sank. Yet it is possible for infants to understand *how* materials like iron and concrete can be made to float. This is possible after the children have made Plasticine boats. Some children will even be able to put their know-how into writing. Meanwhile, all will have acquired knowledge and skills which, in later years, will contribute to their understanding of Archimedes' Principle of buoyancy.

Why does a boat float? A scientist would say that it happens because the vessel can displace, or 'push away', its own weight of water. (Weight, by the way, is thought of as a downward-acting force by scientists.) Displaced water pushes back with a force called upthrust, because it seems to be acting upward on the boat. The magnitude of upthrust is no more nor less than the weight of displaced water. So a boat floats when its weight is balanced by an upthrust. Iron, though, is denser than water. A cubic centimetre of solid iron has more 'heavy stuff' (matter) in it than the equivalent cube of water. Therefore, solid iron cannot displace its own weight in water – so it sinks. But, if the metal is shaped into a thin hollow bowl, it very easily displaces its own weight when put into water – and it floats.

Back to the classroom

Tables were covered with polythene, and each pair of children received a plastic tank nearly filled with lukewarm water. I used the cut-off bottoms of plastic sweet-jars. (These, being disposable, can be obtained for a nominal sum, by asking at a sweet shop.) Each child was given a 25g ball of Plasticine before I introduced the lesson by asking what would happen if the Plasticine were put into the water. Recalling my earlier lesson, when we investigated some materials and objects which floated and sank, the children thought that the Plasticine balls would sink. They did. Then I posed the problem: 'Can the Plasticine be made to float?' Words like 'bowl' and 'boat' were deliberately not mentioned, but I expected that some children would remember our previous experience with a glass jar that could be made to float or sink.

Sally and Cynthia began by breaking their clay into small pieces. Were they thinking that 'lightness' alone would solve the problem? They already knew that objects which felt light in weight often floated. But they had no way of knowing that density, or heavy stuff per unit cube, compared with water, was of utmost importance. Most of the fragments sank, although some shell-like bits actually floated (because, in effect, they were thin shallow boats). I reminded these children that they were required to float all their Plasticine in one piece. Meanwhile, Timothy carefully fashioned a hollow object resembling a Cornish pasty. He hoped it would float, 'because it had air inside'. Quite independently, another boy hit on the same idea. Unfortunately both pasty-like objects sank.

Ian and Molly cheated by sticking their Plasticine to the side of the tank, just on the waterline. Were these children being content with a mere impression of floating? Or were they playing a clever joke, to compensate for failure? Perhaps their attempts were examples of Jean Piaget's 'intuitive thought', through which children accept appearances for reality, and readily accept magical explanations. The 'pasty boats' might also be worth considering in Piagetian terms. Between ages five to seven, infant thinking generally is changing from intuitive to 'concrete operations', whereby a child can tackle certain practical problems on the basis of actual experience. Timothy knew that things with air inside them often floated, but he did not appreciate the importance of volume.

It was interesting to recall an American teacher's experience, where a child 'solved' the problem by fixing a Plasticine 'net' across the water, before resting the remaining clay on the middle. Undoubtedly these problem-solving activities opened windows into the ways that the children thought – a means of enlightenment for an observant teacher. Lisa's answer was to form the clay into a (solid) 'float ring'. John made a cigar-like thing, that he hoped to make lighter by floating it up on end! But several children became boat-builders from the start, though it was hard to tell whether they were aiming for a functional boat, or for something that only resembled a boat. Clare, who was described to me by her teacher as 'creative' – and whose father was clever with machines – became the first child to succeed.

Clare set to work, to produce a thin-walled symmetrical bowl. It floated first time. However there was a little leak in it, so the vessel slowly filled with water and sank. The children found wet Plasticine difficult to manipulate satisfactorily, so I supplied fresh balls of clay when the original material became unworkable. By the end of the lesson most children were making good boats, refining designs by keeping them leak-proof and making thin sides. Some children thought it advisable to make the walls as tall as possible, but most boat-builders preferred a bowl shape. Afterwards, Joanne wrote: 'First I had a little piece and it did not work and then I made it in a boat shape and it did work and I filled in the holes and then I stopped.'

Most children wrote some sentences about the activity, as well as drawing a 'picture record'. A few drawings showed crescent-shaped sectional views, expressing the boat's hollow-ness. Water tanks were, in any case, transparent, but several drawings 'described' their hollow interior spaces too, by omit-ting the tops. (I am sure that little children's drawings consti-tute features that can be 'read' like words.) I encouraged the children to draw in themselves. With a notable exception, the self-portrayals smiled. Tom drew two pictures. In one he had made himself smile, because – as we could see – his boat floated. In the other he grimaced, for the boat had sunk – and he wrote, 'I'm mad.'

Marbles afloat

An infant working to solve the problem of how to make denser-than-water Plasticine float is a step or two along the winding road of first-hand experience and ideas, leading, years later, to an understanding of Archimedes' Principle of buoy-ancy. The principle is clearly stated, at adult level, in just twenty words. It tells us that 'the buoyant force which a fluid exerts on a submerged body is equal to the weight of the fluid displaced'. But a definition is nonsense unless we know its meaning and, more importantly, how it can be useful. Some of the quoted words are uncommon in everyday speech. What are the meanings of 'buoyant', 'fluid', 'exert', 'submerge', 'body' and 'displaced'? What does a scientist mean by 'force'? Yet again we are reminded that every teacher is a language teacher.

What must a child know, before adequate understanding of the principle is possible? A list might include the following: Floating objects are supported by water. An object sinks when water cannot support it enough (but such an object feels lighter under water). The magnitude of the supporting force depends upon the weight of water displaced. An object can only displace its own volume of water. Displaced water 'tries' to push back up. The 'push back force' is called upthrust. There is a contest between the downward pull of gravity (weight) and the buoyant upthrust. Objects sink when gravity 'wins'. Any material can be made to float by getting it to displace enough water. A floating object actually goes down a little – until it has displaced its own volume of water. Meanwhile, the child must learn to conserve weight and volume, on the way to acquiring a concept of density.

Conclusion and evaluation

'What is our problem going to be this week?' asked Timothy. I was facing the infants a week after they tackled the task of getting Plasticine to float. 'You must try to make your boat hold as many marbles as possible,' I told the children. There was excitement as the little plastic tanks of water and 25g clay balls were issued. Then quiet, as most of the children quickly formed shapely boats which floated. Successful children worked confidently, but there were perhaps four or five individuals who failed, still needing help and reassurance. A boy who made a pasty-like object last lesson put two marbles in a Plasticine bowl before squeezing the rim together, completely enveloping the balls in clay. He told me that he wanted to stop the marbles from falling out and to stop the water getting in.

We stopped working for a while, to discuss together the best ways to make the Plasticine boats hold more marbles. Joanne, writing later, said: 'Make the walls higher. Make the walls thinner. Put the marbles in carefully. Put the marbles in the middle. Then make the walls stronger.' Lisa wrote: 'Today I have four marbles in my boat and lots of times it sank.' Peter, a clever boy with spectacles who (the class teacher told me) lacked confidence in himself, made a splendid boat which held six marbles. Nobody managed more than six. The activity continued for half an hour, before I asked the children to write and draw about their experience. Two-thirds of the class began recording, while the remainder continued experimenting. Ian and John stayed with their boats, because (evidently) they did not want to write anything.

On the whole, the class enjoyed reporting their experiments, and responded happily to my suggestion that they include a named portrait of themselves in their pictures. Drawings of the actual clay boats revealed interesting differences in presentation. A few children attempted difficult side-views, representing the clay bowl and its contents realistically. Robert drew a transparent semicircle, with six crayoned marbles arranged formally within – like a smiling mouth. Rachel drew a bird's-eye view of her boat, as if it were hovering (sideways) over the water. Lucy's boat was also transparent, and situated on top of some highly exaggerated waves. But in the cross-sectional drawing by Clare, all the marbles were shown well below the water-line. John's boat was in the act of sinking, with marbles spilling out.

The class teacher told me that the children talked about their work when I was absent. She overheard two boys talking about their bathtime experiences with sponges, which could be made to float or sink. This was after I mentioned 'a stone that floats' (pumice). On another occasion a child described an experiment he did at home with a milk bottle. He found that it supported a lot of weight before sinking. And he figured that, if he had sufficient Plasticine to make a tube shape, it might float with many marbles inside. But I felt that the class had moved as far towards an eventual understanding of floating and sinking as they were able to go at that time. For the fourth lesson, I brought in a box of corks. The children found that their boats held more corks than marbles, 'because corks are lighter than marbles'.

I also introduced a toy deep-sea diver, which could be made to sink and rise in a big tank of water by a child sucking and blowing through a thin tube connected with it. The diver created immediate interest and made a happy climax to the four lessons. Previously, drawings were beginning to lack vitality. But some fine pictures were drawn of the diver. Peter's diver was complete with heavy boots and big round helmet, with a window, and with bubbles rising to the surface of heavily coloured blue water. John wrote: 'You suck the air to make the man go down and you blow the air to make the man come up.' The main trouble with the diver (bought very cheaply at a local shop) was hygiene, because every child was determined to have a go.

How did I evaluate the lessons? The project certainly created intense interest and stimulated thoughtful discussions. Interest was reflected in the children's writing and drawing, and enthusiasm persisted after lessons. Recording provided other opportunities for practising communication skills. *But what science did the children learn?* Most important of all, the children experienced science as an enjoyable problem-solving activity. The children were encouraged to be simple scientists and to think in open-ended ways. Some physical properties of materials were investigated and, although volume and density were never mentioned, the children learned how matter in a material could be redistributed, to affect how well it was supported by water.

Another point of view

Through an act of magic, a primitive huntsman illustrates his desire to find and kill an animal for food. But I have seen the same principle at work among teachers aiming to make a strong cardboard bridge. Knowing little of engineering principles, the non-technical teacher builds a bridge that simply looks like a bridge – and fails, because cardboard is no substitute for stone. Any infants' teacher is familiar with imitative magic. A colleague told me about an infant who had been playing intently with a horseshoe magnet and some steel ball-bearings. Later, when the magnet was put away and the child was required to make Plasticine models, the infant made a clay horseshoe, and looked very puzzled when it failed to attract ball-bearings. After all, it looked like a magnet – therefore it should be a magnet . . .

'Magic' will not turn Plasticine into a real magnet, but it might make Plasticine float. A child knows that anything can be modelled in clay. A boat floats, so why not shape the Plasticine into a boat? And, if the child builds the boat bowl-shaped, it might actually float, by lucky chance . . . The problem is solved, but what science has been learned? (Though magic didn't work for the little girl who made a 'float ring' resembling a solid doughnut.) When I asked the children why their Plasticine floated, they told me 'because it was boat shaped' and 'because it held air'. Answer one might have meant 'because the magic worked'. But answer two held a glimmering of understanding. Many children were impressed by the air-holding capacity of the boat, and they told me that the sides should be as tall and thin as possible. Full understanding would only come with ideas like these.

6
Discovering Magnetism with Younger Juniors – and Student-Teachers

In which magnets 'kiss'

In the autumn term a class of twenty-three seven-to-eight-year-olds were invited to experiment with bar magnets, steel paper-clips, soft-iron tacks and perspex sheets supported upon wooden blocks – forming little 'tables'. It was an experiment to see what these very young children could learn by discovery alone. At first they did not know what to do with the apparatus. I needed to start them working by making suggestions though, later, the children did begin to try out original ideas. One difficulty was that the youngsters had very little previous experience of science in school – and they had not 'done experiments' before. Nevertheless, after about half an hour of enjoyable activity, most of the children had learned something about magnets – so I asked them to write and draw about their discoveries.

With prompting, pairs of children began to appreciate that bar magnets could 'do' different things to each other. A hand-held magnet could be used to push another one across the smooth desk top, without the magnets actually touching. A magnet standing up on end could be pushed over by invisible force, if the second magnet was moved towards it. Also, the magnets pulled together and 'stuck' end-to-end if they were manipulated in other ways. In general discussion, the children were helped to realise that opposite ends of the magnets were different. We noticed that one end (on our *Eclipse* magnets) was marked by a deep dent. So we called the dented end the magnet's 'hole end'. Forces were simply 'pushes' and 'pulls', and the children identified rules, deciding whether a pair of magnets would push or pull each other.

Now it was easy for the children to make drawings of their magnets interacting. They drew red oblongs having single terminal black spots. Even a non-writer could record his newly acquired knowledge in 'picture-writing'. Paul, drawing his magnets head-to-tail, wrote: 'This will go together.' And, after showing the magnets separated and the other way opposed, wrote: 'This will not go together.' His appreciation of magnetic force was shown by ray-like scribblings in the gap between repelling magnets. There was no need to burden the class with words like 'attraction' and 'repulsion', or with a label – such as 'Laws of Magnetism' – for the rules. Celia wrote: 'If you put the end of the magnet with the hole to the other hole in the other magnet they will go together.' The children were making meaningful scientific statements in language that had immediate significance for them.

Other children found that they could make chains of paperclips, without having to interlock the links, if the first clip was dangling from a magnet. Such chains, made on top of the perspex tables, could be pulled along like toy trains if magnet 'engines' were drawn along underneath. But the magnet had to be held as close as possible to the plastic . . . Already the children were gaining the impression that magnetic force could act through other materials. 'If you put some paperclips on top of some plastick and move a magnet under the plastick you can move the paperclips and make a paton.' (The class teacher *sometimes* let the children spell words how they sounded, to encourage the 'flow' of communication.)

Paperclip chain games revealed subtleties of magnetic phenomena. For example, a clip remained weakly magnetised after the magnet was taken away. In fact, the weak clip 'magnet' was often still strong enough to pull another clip. Also, there was a limit to the length of chain possible with a given magnet (although different ends of the magnet might not always support the same number of links). (Once, playing with my son when he was eight years old, I noticed that while connecting a train of clips behind a magnet he said: 'I wonder if the power lasts?' When no extra clips could be taken along, he answered himself by saying a definite 'No.' Then he intrigued me by clustering all his clips near the magnet's end, and said: 'So I'll put them nearer the power.' It's easy to wreck a child's thought by insistence on adult language.)

I taught some children to do an Indian Rope Trick, performed with a paperclip on a length of cotton, and a bar magnet. The free end of the cotton was Sellotaped to the desk, while the magnet was taped to a chair standing on the desk, so that one of the magnet's poles was less than a centimetre away from the nearest part of the clip. Thus the clip was supported in mid air, by being pulled towards the magnet. The children loved this game – and the fun was enhanced when I cut out a paper 'man' and showed the children how 'he' could be passed between the clip and magnet, without causing the erect cotton and clip to collapse. Many individuals tried the trick, and Steve described his results thus: 'If you heald a roll of coton and wind out a bit and tiy a clip to it and put a magnet up above it it will stand up on its own.'

I introduced a pair of plastic toy figures in the forms of a boy and girl. When they were brought together, the models 'kissed', producing delighted laughter. When I asked how the toys worked, the children quickly guessed that there were magnets hidden inside the puppets' heads. Sandra forgot to mention the magnets, when she wrote: 'If you put two children together they kiss each other.' So much had happened within an hour. Slow to initiate their own investigations, the children responded happily to suggestions – and all wanted to share and repeat the activities. This was *guided discovery*: insight coming through free manipulation of materials. There was no need for me to do much direct informing. Appropriate questions, put to individuals or to the whole class, evoked relevant facts and words from the pupils themselves.

Would the interest be maintained next week?

The meaning of discovery

The first Americans knew America before Columbus 'discovered' the continent. Discovery means finding something not previously known – to the discoverer. It is often confused with inventing. All learning is discovery when ideas are being met for the first time. When, listening to a boring lecture on 'Atoms', it dawns on us that an iron ball is mostly empty space – and that all the steel ships in the world might, conceivably, be crushed into a thimble – we are making a profound personal discovery that shatters previous thinking about the nature of the universe. 'Discovery method' in teaching is simply wise teaching. Ideas cannot be packed into minds, but the teacher can create an exciting atmosphere (of words, pictures, feelings and things) from which a motivated learner can derive ideas.

Magnets are particularly useful for a teacher who believes that children learn best through free activity with materials. They look simple, are pleasant to handle, and exhibit forces as startling in their effects as magic. Magnets seem alive. (Is that why teachers who are unhappy with physics, but who like nature study, don't mind experimenting with magnets?) A week after twenty-three first-year juniors were introduced to practical magnetism, the children felt confident enough to explore the possibilities of their own ideas. To an adult, their discoveries might have appeared trivial. Not so to the astonished children. Penny wrote: 'If you put a pin in a yogurt pot and put the magnet under it and turn it over the pin will stay there!' And Don informed us, 'If you want to make an umbrella you nid a maganite and french coffee lid . . .'

Other children were happy to recapitulate what they had learned from the previous lesson. Suzanne recorded, 'When I put the magnet together sometimes it go's but sometimes it do's not go . . .' While a child who had created a manikin with paperclips and a magnet captioned a picture of herself experimenting with, 'If you put some magnets to touch with a hole in it (the dent indicating the north pole) they will push.' There were many drawings of the magnets festooned with paperclip chains, and illustrations of the magnets 'going' and 'not going' together. I found it was best to listen to the children's words for what was happening. Their terms and phrases came from struggling to express actual experience, and would do until they were able to relate their language to the official language of scientists. Textbook science belongs to later years.

It is important for children who are learning about magnets to feel the invisible pushes and pulls which act in such mysterious ways across space and through certain 'non-magnetic' materials like water, wood, glass and plastics. Scientists describe forces like electrostatic attraction and repulsion, gravity and magnetism as 'acting at a distance'. Such forces do not involve bodies touching each other. Using strong magnets, a child experiences magnetic pulling as 'stickiness'. And forcing two like poles together is like plunging into very viscous syrup. Feeling these powerful influences through 'muscle sense' gives never-to-be-forgotten kinesthetic pleasure. Not infrequently, the sensation provokes delighted laughter. But only thus do children come to know magnetism as an entity more wonderful than the mere performance of magnets.

A popular magic trick is the suspension of a pretty girl in mid air. Levitation is an intriguing idea that can be demonstrated with magnets. One way is to use a pair of 8cm diameter ceramic 'ring magnets' found inside old television sets. The almost black pottery-like substance is barium ferrite. These magnets, having poles on their surfaces, are powerful, and their force does not deteriorate – but they are brittle and must not be dropped. I gave the children a 10cm tall fat wooden 'peg' mounted upon a wooden base, and I suggested that they try to make the rings push each other apart, while 'caught' upon the peg. James wrote: 'If you put two round magnets on to a stand they push away. If you put them the other way round they pull together . . .' Barium ferrite 'bricks' could be used to levitate parts of a 'hovertrain'.

The children were fascinated by my 'Force Field Box', inside which magnets' invisible force fields could be made visible, using iron filings, nails, or paperclips as 'field lines of force indicators'. A teaspoonful of fine iron filings, or a handful of small paperclips or nails were sealed inside a plain rectangular transparent plastic lunchbox, using Sellotape. Magnets held against the box revealed their forces through their beautiful effects on the materials inside. Filings, nails or clips were forced to 'bristle' like porcupines' spines, or to form curved lines, describing ways the magnetic flux interacted. But, to the children, these wonders were simply more of their magnets' miraculous effects. The children only appreciated that the filings made patterns, 'If you put to magnets at the top and have a box off nails you can make a paten . . .'

Uninhibited drawing and writing stimulated the children to organise their thinking, thereby facilitating powers to communicate their latest knowledge. Communication is an extension and reinforcement of the discovery process. A scientist's work is incomplete until he has formulated and published his work for critical review. 'Publishing' children's records on the classroom wall can be an important part of elementary science teaching method – but the children must be permitted to express what *they* think. Anthony saw that steel nuts were only pulled together like a train when they were touching and in line with the magnet. In one drawing he showed the magnet and nuts 'train' going together. And in a second drawing he showed the nuts spread apart and some distance from the magnet, with the caption: 'These will not go together.'

Anthony's drawings showed a promising flair for visual design. Indeed, children's 'picture writing' is frequently boldly expressive (although we do have to learn to 'read' it). Drawings of the filings, clips or nails in the Force Field Box were clearly suggestive of the patterns of resultant fields of interacting magnets – which the children would study in detail in later years. *We could only hope that those future lessons would hold more interest and have more meaning as a result of the children's leisurely activity then.* Teaching this way sorely taxes one's reserves of nervous energy. But the children generally appreciate our efforts, and the personal satisfaction is immensely rewarding. Mary shall have the last word. Next to her cluttered picture, she wrote: 'This is me doing some magnets. I like doing them very much.'

How would my own non-specialist student primary science teachers respond to similar opportunities?

Magnetism and imagination

'This was, as far as I can remember, my first real experience with magnets. I think the most impressive thing I learnt from them was the peculiar sensation one feels when two magnets are pulling towards one another. It is a weirdly indescribable feeling. A feeling which seems in a way to sap all strength from one's body, and leaves one motionless. To me, the drawing together of two magnets was as if all the forces of the Earth were pulling together, and gravitating at one point. What also fascinated me was how one can build up tin tacks on a magnet. Their shapes and positions made me think of some abstract sculpture standing in the early morning light on a winter's day. One of the sculptures erected reminded me a great deal of a poem by Ted Hughes, called "The Horses" – in which the poet sees ten horses standing on a hillside in the cold, silvery light of dawn, like statues "megalith still".'

This piece of creative writing was done by a non-scientist student at what was Saint Mary's (women's) College of Education, Cheltenham, during a one and a half hour period, when with nineteen others she was invited to experiment freely with a wide range of magnetic materials. I wished to know what sorts of investigations, games and other activities the students would initiate themselves. Also, would their shared experience convince them of magnets' potential value to stimulate imaginative thinking? *I believe that teachers can only arouse and encourage their pupils' creative powers, when they themselves have been inspired.* Imagination is as essential to scientists as to artists. Einstein went so far as to say that he thought imagination to be more important than knowledge. Teachers learn that if ideas won't appeal, they must – in common with the ad man and publicity agent – try to stimulate the imagination.

My students responded with such enthusiasm that I would like to describe some of their ideas, as of possible value to other teachers wishing to attempt similar work with children. Brenda recorded: 'I put a small nail and a paperclip together (ends-on to a bar magnet's north pole) and slowly moved a magnet towards them, keeping equidistantly from both. The magnet first pulled the clip towards it. The clip was lighter than the nail. Then I marked the distance that it had pulled the nail, and did the same experiment again, using the magnet's south pole. The south pole attracted the nail the greatest distance.' Celia's version was neater. She rested a paperclip broadside-on, alongside – but not touching – one of a bar magnet's poles. Then she measured how close the magnet had to be, before it attracted the clip. The distance varied with each pole, so she concluded that one pole was weaker than the other.

Celia's experiment can be improved in several ways. She might have put the clip and magnet on to a sheet of glass, to reduce friction, and placed the glass over a piece of graph paper to facilitate measurement. She might also have inquired whether the powers of all magnets seemed to differ at opposite ends. And she might have carried out tests to compare the 'strengths' of a whole batch of similar bar magnets. With guidance, these simple numerical tests can be undertaken by younger juniors. My own version of the test is to use a pack of playing cards. The experimenter measures through how many arbitrary 'card units' the pole of a magnet will attract a 'standard paperclip'. The playing card test is easy to do, and the results can be quickly recorded in bar-graph form. Then – for abler children – the question of how to measure the thickness of a single playing card will provide an interesting diversion into the mathematics of averages.

Several students compared the powers of bar magnets to attract chains of soft iron tacks (from Woolworth's). But Joan's extension of Brenda's and Celia's test was very interesting. Joan found that the distance over which a magnet would attract a 4cm steel nail depended on how the nail was approached. The magnet needed to come closer to the point than to the head of the nail. The nail was pulled the greatest distance when it was approached from the middle. A simple explanation of this easily-confirmed observation – for the students – would be as follows: In order to attract iron or steel, a magnet must induce magnetism of opposite polarity in the metal. The more mass of metal there is to be affected, the stronger is the induced force. Since the nail's weight was constant, and friction between the nail and a sheet of glass remained the same, it followed that the nail was attracted over the furthest distance, when the greater massiveness of its middle part came within range of the magnet's influence.

(However, it is unwise to attempt theoretical explanations when working with primary school children. Accurate observation, verified by careful repetition, recorded simply as 'What We Found Out', provides excellent concrete knowledge upon which a secondary science teacher can build when the theory is expounded in after years.) Indeed, observations of magnetism can be very baffling. A student observed that: 'If two like poles are placed facing each other, there seems to be an invisible barrier pushing them apart. If a piece of iron (such as one of the so-called keepers, supplied with a pair of bar magnets) is placed between the repelling poles, the magnets will stick together – although their strength of magnetism is not very strong.' This strange fact is not at all easy to explain. Meanwhile, another student began a poem: 'Attracting, repelling: constructing, destroying: joining together with a will of their own. Balancing, shattering: supporting, refuting all that was built with a single touch . . .'

Fascinated by magnetic attraction and repulsion, Sarah wrote: 'Two people each held a ring magnet in one hand. The force with which they were pulled together was unbelievable – very strong, willing, and pulling: as though there was a link between the two. One person could control the action of the arm of the other person, raising it by raising their magnet.' And:

'One person held a magnet in each hand, but the magnets repelled each other and the person found she couldn't push the magnets together, although she exerted a tremendous force. She could feel the tension in her muscles. Even when she put down the magnets, the feeling of not being able to control the hands wasn't forgotten.' After moving a magnet beneath a transparent box containing iron filings, a student wrote that the filings 'stood up like fur', and animated filings patterns looked as if 'they were trees being blown in the wind'.

These recorded experiences and impressions typify what anyone can find out about magnetism through patient play with the materials; and several of the examples clearly illustrate the role of the imagination in learning at first hand. Elementary secondary school physics books give only a limited account of magnetism. The 'essentials' are reckoned to be a brief history of magnetism, the importance of the compass in navigation, magnetic and non-magnetic materials, the Laws of Magnetism, and a simple look at magnetic fields. All these important ideas are fascinating enough, but fostering a leisurely and playful familiarity with magnets reveals so much more. It is the details in physics – as in all science – which most excite a sense of wonder. The details are not necessarily difficult to see, if habits of careful observation are encouraged and pursued. There is time in primary schools to appreciate the 'little things'. But theories to explain them must wait.

7
Three Junior Science Case Histories

Pulses as timers

Time is a human invention. In nature there is duration, enfolding cycles of physical conditions, to which natural forms have adapted. Therefore, in Britain, the hedgehog's instincts – whatever they might be – 'anticipate' winter's austerity; so the creature gets fat and looks for a place to hibernate. A baby howls to be fed, because the prolongation of duration, without sorely needed sustenance, signals hunger pangs. What we in our adult wisdom recognise as a toddler's impatience is perhaps the child's dawning appreciation of duration – a key which will unlock a concept of time. Soon the child can understand and use words and phrases like 'dinner time', 'time for school', and 'bedtime' – words that are points plotted along a succession of days. Thus language makes possible the numerical subdivisions of our experience into hours, minutes and seconds – the function of clocks.

Timing is an essential scientific process, well within the capacity of middle primary children. So I chose 'Timing Things' as a topic for a class of thirty-six eight- and nine-year-olds. Knowing how much young children like experimenting upon themselves, an aim of my first lesson was to teach them something about the pulse, and how its beating could be detected and counted. I described a pulse as 'throbbing', felt when blood is pumped in surges through an artery ('blood pipe'). After demonstrating how a wrist pulse can be felt, I encouraged the children to discover their own. Few found this easy. A child (who wasn't very lively and felt cold) was unable to feel either her own (weak) pulse, or mine. I had the impression that she might be listening, rather than feeling.

I therefore showed the children how to make two types of 'pulsometer', with which they might watch magnified movements produced in time with their wrist pulses. Happily, many children were able to find their pulses with these simple instruments.

Pulsometer model one was merely a piece of paper drinking straw, pinched at the bottom and standing vertically on a large drawing pin which served as a base. Model two – which we felt worked better – was made by fixing the pin sideways through the middle of a full-length straw. In both cases the wrist was upturned and held level, and the pulsometer was rested on it and moved about until it began to shake slightly, rhythmically, denoting that the pulse was found. Children having weak pulses were able to observe better results with the pulses of their friends. But, while the children worked, I saw that one little girl, misunderstanding my instructions, was actually trying to pin a straw to her wrist! When dealing with children, and – I believe – with people in general, one should be prepared for the incredible, especially where safety is a factor.

Later, I distributed paper, pencils and crayons, and asked the children to write and draw about what they had learned. Monica wrote: 'The pulse is a beat from the hart. The heart bumps the bloud into the vanes which makes the beat in yore rist. To find the pulse, find the radius the bone directle in line with the thome. Then find the artery in yore rist. The pulse is in the middle.' Andrew wrote: 'The pulse is a blood stream being pumped by the heart. The heart pumps the blood through a tube called the artery. To find my pulse I felt gently with my finger tips until I felt a light throbbing. Then I marked with my ink pen where my pulse was. Next I started to make a pulsometer. First I got a straw and stuck the drawing pin in it. Then by placing the head of the pin on my pulse. Soon the pulsometer began to quiver and that meant that blood was being pumped through the artery.'

Several drawings showed the blood vessels under the skin, and there was one notable attempt at an anatomical diagram, with 'bone', 'arterys' and a precise point for the pulse labelled. Tom wrote: 'If you feel just under your jaw you will find another pulse.' The success of my lesson was in the amount of interest engendered. My failure was in not getting on to my 'Timing Things' theme. Also, I began to wonder whether I had said too much about anatomy.

My objectives for lesson two, a week later, were (*a*) to reveal individual differences in the pulse rate, by exploiting the inadequacy of pulses as timers – thereby (*b*) stressing the need for a reliable standard timer. Unfortunately I had assumed that most of the children would be able to draw graphs, showing their group's differing pulse rates for the timing tasks I provided. Actually, half the class found the graph-making difficult. But, in conclusion, a child wrote: 'Timing things with our pulses is not a good thing, because all our pulses are different and it is much better to use a stopwatch. A stopwatch is a watch you can stop when you like and start when you like.'

I provided three timing tasks, each to be done by two groups of children. The first was to time how long a candle flame stayed alight under an inverted jam jar. The second was to time water draining from a holed yogurt pot into a coffee jar. The third was to find the time between pressing down a sucker-and-spring delayed-action 'pop up' toy, and its dramatically climactic leap into the air. Of the latter, David wrote: 'A pop-up toy works by being pushed down, then the suction grips and the spring forces it up, until the suction lets go and the toy jumps.' Gaye was intrigued by the chemical changes associated with burning. She wrote: 'When the candle burns out it leaves a black mark made by the smoke settling at the top of the glass.' *These incidental interests were bonuses in the children's scientific learning.*

In spite of the difficulties I shared with the children during these two lessons, two consequences were well documented in the children's records. Many individuals could now feel and count their pulse, and there was a general awareness that pulses were too variable to be of much use as timers. The class was ready for the introduction of a standard timing device.

A mouse named Fred

The trouble with direct teaching is that children tend to remember what you say. Summarising lesson three on the topic of 'Timing Things', Steve wrote: 'First we did some revision. Mr Ward asked us some questions on what we'd done in the last two weeks. Then he got a stop clock out and timed a minute. We found out how many pulse beats we had in one minute. Mine was 93. That was the practice run. Now we did the same thing again. This time mine was 102. It was higher because we were excited. Mr Ward decided to count the practice run because it was our true pulse.' Was I really as dogmatic as Steve's terse 'explanation' made me out to be? Probably.

Naturally a teacher is pleased to be quoted by his students. What worried me was realising how great was my responsibility to tell the class the 'correct' thing. Only I knew how arbitrary had been my hurried decision to count only the 'practice' pulses.

According to the children, their pulses varied between Jaqueline's 41 and Alison's 144. The class average was about 90. These rates, timed with the stopclock, were incorporated in a class graph. Uncomfortably aware that 90 beats per minute seemed high, I felt that we needed to discuss the effect of excitement on the heart's activity. Tony later wrote: 'It was great fun and we found something out, because when we get excited our heart beats faster, and it is the heart which makes the pulse beat, it makes the pulse beat faster too.' Some children were still unable to feel their own pulses. Jane's record says that she could not find hers, so she listened to Jonathan Smith's heart. She put her ear to his chest. Indeed, listening directly to another child's heart is probably the easiest way for youngsters to take a 'pulse'. Jonathan's 'hart beated 88 times'.

The stopclock created enormous interest. Ben wrote, 'A timer can time things. It works by things inside what make it tic. If you want to run around and you want to see how long it takes, all you have to do is pull a lever.' Many children drew the stopclock, enabling me to study how closely its external features had been observed. In fact its face was divided into sixty minutes (or seconds) and clearly marked in multiples of five. There was a minute hand, and a seconds 'sweep' hand. Half the drawings I have before me now are carefully observed copies of the actual clock. The others mostly resemble clocks in everyday use. Perhaps the trouble was that I used only the one stopclock – although it was in each child's line of sight. *Nevertheless, accurate observation is the most vital scientific skill to be stressed and encouraged.*

Now that the children were used to elementary timing operations, I wished to end the series of four lessons with a particularly memorable experience. We began by repeating the candle-under-a-jar activity from lesson two. In that lesson the children had used their pulses to time the survival of a flame under an inverted jam jar. This time the children – again working in groups – used a stopclock. The jars used were identical, and the candles employed were as nearly equal in height as I could manage. The children found that the standardised times for their candles varied between 9 and 15 seconds. This was my cue to start a discussion on what the 'correct' result might be. A few children realised that, in fact, we had no way of telling whether any of the results were correct. One or two children appreciated the meaning of averaging results, but on this occasion I did not press the idea.

I was also keen for the class to see that the usual reason stated for the candle going out was wrong. Usually people, and textbooks, say that the candle goes out after using up the air. Sometimes, more scientifically literate persons say 'oxygen' instead of air. Both versions of the ancient explanation were given by the eight- and nine-year-olds. Some books, including ones currently in print, go to great lengths in 'demonstrating' through well-drawn pictures that twenty per cent of the air (the total proportion of oxygen) is consumed. They do this by putting the candle into shallow water, and then showing that, as the flame goes out, the water level rises one-fifth of the way into the jar – supposedly displacing all the oxygen. One obvious objection to this explanation is to ask: 'What happens to the carbon dioxide produced by combustion?'

Now for the climax. As Jenny wrote: 'Mr Ward said I have brout one of my little friends to experiment for us. Mr Ward's little friend was a mouse.' I said to the children: 'If the candle used up all the oxygen or air, what should happen to the mouse, if it were under the jar when the flame went out?' Unanimously, the cry was: 'It would die!' Then I produced a very big sweet jar, and put it in an elevated place, where everybody could see it. I lit a tall candle and put it, together with the mouse, underneath the jar. At the same moment I started the stopclock. A number of children were visibly apprehensive, while the flame sickened to pale blue, and went out. But the mouse stayed just as lively as ever, exploring its glass prison, or standing up against the candle.

Under my suggested heading of 'Why does the candle under the jar go out?' Andrew wrote: 'Today we were finding out how long a candle would last under a glass jar. We had a practice go at first and our table had 12 seconds. Then we had the real one and we timed it with a stopclock and we got 9 seconds. Then we had an experiment with a mouse in a (much larger) jar, with a candle. After 40 seconds the candle went out, but there was still enough air left in the jar to keep the mouse alive.' In their book entitled *Candles* (Macdonald Educational), authors John Bird and Dorothy Diamond write: 'Dr Kempa says (with experimental evidence) in *Science Teaching Techniques No. 12*, that candle flames do not use up all the oxygen, but only one third of it. This leaves fourteen per cent oxygen in the jar; a candle will not burn with less oxygen than this, he says.'

The reader might disapprove of my use of the mouse. Of course, I knew that the mouse would not die. But the children did not know – and it was important for them not to know for sure, because I wanted to stage-manage the situation, for purposes of child motivation, memorability, and dramatic build up. I have already admitted that a few of the children were apprehensive although, without my being too convincing at that stage, I did take care to inform the children beforehand that I would not let the mouse suffer or actually die . . . Suzy must have the last word: 'Today we had a clock and a jar and some candle and we had experiments and we had a mouse in a box and we had a big jar and we put the mouse in the jar and we put the candle in. The flame went out after forty seconds and the mouse was alive and he was happy and I was happy because the mouse was happy and the mouse whose name was Fred.'

The children were urged not to attempt the experiment themselves.

Yogurt pot telephones

'First of all we made the telephone and went outside to try them, which was great fun. When we were outside we were speeking through them. I said radio control do you reseve me, do you reseve me and the answer I got was I reseve you aeroplane flight number 1 hundred and sixty.'

These actual words reflected the interest and excitement of 'The Yogurt Pot Telephone Project' that I organised with a class of forty second- and third-year juniors. The work, in four hour-long lessons, was continued over four consecutive Tuesday afternoons. The children were divided into groups of four, and their practical work was initially directed through the use of a work card. I began by asking the children what they already knew about sound.

They appreciated that sound was associated with vibration, and that something called sound waves could travel to their ears. Each group leader was given a copy of the work card, and one member of each group collected from me about twenty metres of string, some scissors, and three yogurt pots having 0.2cm diameter holes bored in the centres of their bottom ends. Giving out the apparatus was noisy because I gave the materials to individuals, one after the other. (Of course, I should have put everything out in complete kits beforehand.) But the class soon settled down. So I opened the door leading on to the playground, and let the groups go out into the spacious field beyond. There was simply not enough room for forty yogurt pot telephonists inside the building!

The work card instructed the children to stretch the string between the yogurt pots, before speaking into one pot while another person listened through the 'receiver'. All soon found that the telephones carried quiet voices better than the air. Nicholas wrote, 'When we moved a pot on the string it made a funny noise in the other pot on the other end of the string. We then tapped on the string. It made a funny noise. Then we put out fingers on the string and rubbed. It made a noise like felt rubbing but louder.' (Perhaps I ought to have asked the children to find more precise words than 'funny' to describe the sounds.) No drawings were shown to the children, but their own pictorial impressions of the happenings revealed a charming range of styles. One boy actually managed to draw himself in the act of sliding a pot along the taut string – to produce a rasping noise at the receiving end.

Several drawings in pencil and crayon, or coloured felt pens, depicted groups of 'matchstick' children, very like the figures painted by the late L. S. Lowry. Two colourful pictures by girls showed bird's-eye views of a three-way telephone system, in which the scientific record was translated into sheer pattern-work, complete with willow trees and picturebook 'flowers'. These contrasted with other children's attempts to represent the details of the experiments as realistically as possible. The three-way system presented the artists with the problem of how to indicate the third dimension. (There was no difficulty in showing the side view of the simpler two-way system in action.) In one of the pictures we were meant to be looking downward on to the work in progress – but all that we could see of the experimenters was heads, arms, and the toes of shoes.

Here are some more verbatim reports. Sue: 'I thought that the wind was important. It was better to do it in a space alone if you wanted more volume.' David: 'We joined the third carton on the string to the rest. We found that it only worked if you held it taut and straight in the air at ear level. It is all very interesting. I never thought that you could hear through them – but I could very well hear what Melaine was saying. Her voice was crisp and clear.' Pam 'could not hear around corners because the string was rubbing against the wall and stopped it vibrating'. There were occasional disruptions, as when 'somebody ran into it (the string) and got it all tangled up'. Some children needed to continue their writing and drawing in extra time provided by the class teacher.

Lesson two began with a discussion on the work so far. Words, such as 'vibrate', 'pitch', 'conductor', 'transmit' and 'taut' were defined and written upon the blackboard. 'After that,' wrote Gwen, 'we asked Suzanne to take one end of the telephone and go out to the other side of the playground. Mrs Lewis (the class teacher) spoke through the other end, she said "3RO is a very naughty class", at first Suzanne heard it quite well. Phillip then suggested "Would it work with the door closed?" Mrs Lewis tried it she said "Can you hear me now?" Suzanne could not hear anything, so we opened the door and Mrs Lewis said again "Can you hear me now?" Suzanne said yes.'

As a variation on the two-way system I tied both a large and a small yogurt pot at one end. Robert recorded, 'We done an experiment on yogurt pot telephones. Mr Ward spoke through the little one up to Michael with the big telephone and Mr Ward sent Humpty Dumpty up the line. Michael did not hear him very well. So Mr Ward tryed the big telephone this time Michael heard and he said Humpty Dumpty. Catherine came and tryed through the big one. Michael heard this time and said it. Michael said the big one was better than the small.' Lesson two was organised as a class lesson, with children assisting demonstrations. In conclusion: 'We did an experiment on the hart. We found that if you put a big yogurt pot to your hart somebody can hear it.'

During the second lesson I extended the scope of the activities covered by the children in lesson one, while I fully intended to develop subsequent work away from the ideas on the work card. Thus I was proceeding like the teacher who, having started a project with class activities 'structured' by the suggestions on a work card (and having, thereby, gained in self-confidence), responds to the children's revealed interests, and begins to develop more original work. I have always found that young children enjoy talking about what the textbooks call human biology. I thought that, to use a yogurt pot as a variety of 'stethoscope' would trigger off the children's interest in the heart – and in this expectation I was not to be disappointed.

Beating hearts

A 'Lunar Zoomer' was the name we gave to a plastic tube consisting of many ring-formed corrugations. It was designed to be whirled around very fast, to produce beautiful 'wind-whistling' musical sounds. If you twirled the tube faster, the pitch of the note emitted went higher – probably to one of the harmonic tones of the note sounded when the Zoomer was swung more slowly.

However, we found another use for the toy. Used in a quiet place, it served as a stethoscope for listening to children's heart beats. While I was working with forty second- and third-year juniors in class 3RO on 'The Yogurt Pot Telephone Project', I noticed that, if a family-size yogurt pot was held with its open end against a person's chest, a child listening against the bottom of the pot could hear the person's heart beating. That was the climax of lesson two.

Lesson three was dedicated to listening for and counting heart beats. Several children brought their Woolworth's Lunar Zoomers into school. I took along one of the guinea-pigs we kept at college for students' use in teaching. (I often used to say that our laboratory animals worked as hard on teaching practice as the students!) The lesson began with the children working in ten groups, using big yogurt pots or Lunar Zoomers to listen to one another's hearts. During the listening, it was necessary to keep everybody very quiet indeed. Some children found using the 'stethoscopes' difficult, and they were encouraged to put their ears to partners' chests, to listen directly to the heart sounds. Then we were ready to carry out an experiment in simple physiology.

I asked each group to choose a child to be its 'test subject'. Another child in the group was to do the listening. I timed a minute while, absolutely quiet, the children waited for the 'listeners' to practise counting the heart beats. That was our trial run. When I felt reasonably confident that heart beats could be counted with some accuracy, I timed another minute to let the children record the rates of their 'subject' persons, before a lively run around the playground.

In fact, all the children wanted to run around the playground together! As soon as everybody was back in the classroom and settled down, I timed another minute for listeners to count the subjects' pulses after the run. Seven minutes later, I organised another massed pulse-taking. The discipline was absolutely essential.

Here are the results of ten groups' counting:

Before running	After running	Seven minutes later
53	90	48
90	100	90
60	90	64
83	131	83
55	110	90
64	80	76
60	164	100
26	57	62
52	89	47
142	101	60

Discussing these results afterwards, the children appreciated that, in general, vigorous activity increased the heart rate – but that some of the counts were probably unreliable. Nobody had any difficulty in translating group findings into bar graphs. One of the graphs showed a fourth column, indicating a heart rate of 256! It was the pulse of Pip Squeak the guinea-pig, whom the children adored. Commented Jane: 'Pip Squeak's heart beat is high and sounds like a clock ticking. I think it sounds higher than a human's heart beat because it is smaller and the sound would be louder and in a higher tone. Pip Squeak's heart beats 256 times per minute. We used a Lunar Zoomer to listen with.' When Pip Squeak was held, the children could, of course, actually feel its heart beating.

A number of drawings depicting Pip Squeak and the children suggested that representing relative sizes of the animal and themselves presented technical problems – although sometimes it seemed that size of the object represented might be related to the amount of interest it aroused. On listening to the guinea-pig's heart, a girl – whose drawing was quite well-proportioned – wrote that she thought the 256 beats were so high in number, because the heart was small 'and there was so little blood to pump'. Earlier, in lesson three, I had asked the children to point to where they thought their hearts might be. The results were fascinating, indicating supposed locations all over the middle and upper chest and abdomen. So I introduced lesson four by showing the children an anatomical demonstration model of the trunk of a man.

The model (which teachers could borrow from a secondary school) was full scale, and could be 'dissected' simply by pulling out the pegged-together simulated organs and tissues. I was a little worried though, because one side of the manikin's face was as if cut away, revealing a naked eyeball. Of course I covered the head with a blanket. Nevertheless, when the model was shown to the children, they virtually demanded to see all! Reluctantly I showed them the modelled raw face – and I was disturbed to notice a girl go pale, before leaving the room. (There will surely be several points of view about what I did.) But the children were intrigued to see the model heart, which I was able to remove from its easily noted normal position on the dummy. One child drew it, indicating its subdivisions and valves.

During the same lesson, the children were thrilled to use a real stethoscope, borrowed from college. And they were interested by the stethoscope's history – summed up in a paragraph cut from *Reveille* magazine. Its French inventor, Dr Laennec, needed an instrument to enable him to listen to ladies' chests without causing embarrassment. He began in 1816 by experimenting with a rolled newspaper, but soon refined his idea by devising a wooden tube having a tapering interior. But the good doctor, after so considerately minding the ladies' modesty, was still the butt of hostile criticism. His contemporaries – no doubt mingling envy with their righteousness – complained that Laennec had no right to listen to God's own secrets. Therefore his stethoscope became nicknamed 'The Devil's Trumpet'.

Happy Landings

Aiming to investigate parachutes with a large class of fourth-year juniors, I presented groups with a work card suggesting some ways to do it. I will let the children describe in their own words how their 'test' parachutes were constructed and used.

Andrew wrote: 'In this experiment we made parachutes. One was 20^2cm and the other 30^2cm. They were made of tissue paper.' Fiona wrote that each parachute required four lengths of cotton, some Sellotape and a marble. 'We stuck the cotton on to each corner and then we tied the marble on to the ends of the cotton – and to keep it secure we stuck it with Sellotape.' Thus groups of children made a pair of parachutes, each of a pair different in canopy area, but both loaded with the same masses as 'weights'.

Fiona went on to say: 'I stood on my desk and Deborah my friend handed me the parachutes. I got them both at the same height and let them go. I found that the smallest one fell first. All my table tried it, to see if we had the same result and we did.' Naturally I warned the children about the danger of falling off desk tops, but since we needed some height through which to drop the parachutes, I took a calculated risk. It might be appropriate to notice how the excitement of a little scientific activity can lead to practice in the writing of accurate eye-witness reports, complementing the purely creative function of writing English. Also note that all Fiona's friends had a go, before reaching their general conclusion.

The children were encouraged to describe the motion of their falling chutes. Andrew's were coloured green and blue, the blue being the larger. He found that 'The green one went down quicker than the blue. The green floated down in circles, while the blue one floated down in gentle swoops.' Attention to details stimulated imaginative description. None of the parachutes fell steadily at first . . . Steve reported, 'We made a hole in the top (of the parachute) and then we made it bigger. We found that the bigger the hole the less the parachute sways. Our group found that the holes were put in parachutes to steady them, and also that the man in the parachute will not sway and be sick.' Andre Garnerin (1769–1823), inventor of the parachute, found that a hole in the canopy helped to stabilise his descents.

Garnerin reasoned that a perfect dome-shaped parachute would fall until the force of its weight balanced the resisting force of compressed air trapped beneath the canopy. Then, he figured, the parachute – in a still atmosphere – should hover 'without ever ascending or descending'. But he learned from experience that the air always found an imperfect edge of the chute, under which it spilt, causing relatively higher pressure on the opposite part of the canopy, a process that started the dreaded oscillation. Thereafter, as the parachute continued to fall, air flowed alternately from opposite parts, producing fiercer vibration, until the helpless passenger (in his basket) might be swung up almost on a level with the canopy itself. No wonder that Garnerin was often painfully sick after his daring performances.

I remember reading about a para-balloon device designed to rescue US airmen who bailed out over North Vietnam. It was possible to keep the special parachute aloft by heating the air inside, using a gas-burner. The idea was to remain in the sky, above gunfire range, until hooked aboard a transport plane. This 'sky-hook' method has been used to catch instrument packages parachuted from space satellites. One of the children wrote: 'We decided to go outside. So we ran with the parachute and let it go, expecting it to go in the air. But the strings kept breaking at the force of the wind.' When I was a child we sought rising air currents against house gables. There it was possible to release tissue paper parachutes bearing cardboard manikins, which rose like balloons. Garnerin saw children playing a similar game in Paris.

A comparatively recent development is the Para-Commander 'lobstertail' competition chute, a complex slotted cloth 'wing', cleverly steered down amongst admiring crowds at summer air shows. An earlier idea was the Rogallo Wing, a device of fabric and shroud lines, designed to swell and act aerodynamically as a lift-sustaining wing when thrust through the air by a propeller. With its application, an incredibly simple 'flying jeep' was produced. But currently we see the Rogallo Wing principle mounted on the paperdart-like framework of the daredevil hang gliders. Digging much further back into history, we find a story about a girl would-be suicide, who jumped off the Clifton Suspension Bridge into the Avon Gorge, near Bristol. She was saved by the parachute effect of her voluminous skirts!

For extracurricular assignments the children in my class found out about how parachutes can be steered; their use in the American and Russian space programmes; and how they can be used to act as brakes on jet aircraft on landing, and on cars which have accelerated rapidly during drag racing. 'To steer the parachute, a parachutist pulls the cords on the side in which he wants to go. This reduces the parachute in size to about twenty feet diameter and so pushes the air out on that side.' Derek, writing about flying squirrels, said that: 'They use a parachute system to glide from tree to tree. They have folds of skin in between their legs. These folds, called membranes, spread while the animal is gliding. The skin traps air, causing the squirrel to float gently to his destination.' Two girls chose to write about the heart's 'parachute valves' (mitral and bicuspid).

As a climax to our work on parachutes (which was part of a topic study on 'Flight'), I invited children to bring pram wheel 'go-karts' into school. Two turned up, together with old umbrella 'air brakes' that we were going to test. I have some beautiful coloured drawings of children working with the go-karts. 'Tony and I sat in a go-kart and then Colin, John and Mark gave us a push without the umbrellas and went 32 metres, but when we did it again with the umbrella we went 24 metres that means the umbrella fills with air and slows you down.' Terry, a less academically able child, invented 'The Postman Help'. His drawing showed a post van at a tower block of flats. An ejector device shot the mail-bag high in the air. Then a red parachute opened, and the gently descending bag was caught by a net projecting from the tenth floor.

8
An Ideas Bank of
Suggestions for Lessons

The purpose of this chapter is not only to provide ideas for teachers who are searching for activities to meet their preconceived needs, but also to give some inspiration to teachers who are not certain about what their precise needs of the moment might be. The previous chapters about key concepts that cover the whole area of possible concern in primary science education (pages 15–36) can also be used for the same purpose.

The ideas are deliberately kept brief, in order to stimulate original thinking about how the bare suggestions may be attempted in practice. Two of the sections included here refer to widely-ranging topics. The other two sections are intended to illustrate how particular themes might be dealt with in both depth and breadth, to involve several subject areas.

Human biology for juniors

Everyone is interested in themselves. It is only natural. That is an important reason why human biology appeals to even very young children. Boys and girls are nearly always curious to discover how their bodies work. Adults are sometimes rather morbid about this, and will gossip for hours on ailments and operations. But it is healthier to be well informed about the workings of our precious human machinery.

Juniors can approach the science without trespassing too much on secondary curricula. They can be guided to observe their bodies' needs, structures and actions intelligently, as a splendid preparation for secondary work. But, school subjects apart, accurate biological self-knowledge is essential for healthy attitudes to the body and its functions. Some teachers will be happy to let appropriate sex education happen incidentally.

In practice it is perhaps best to organise a few related activities for every child to do so that all can contribute to summarising discussions. It is incredible how much biological information a large class can provide – if a teacher is wise enough to let the children do some of the teaching. Take care though that 'facts' are correct. Books for the nine to thirteen age range should provide a teacher with essential background material, if needed.

Ideas

1 Let the children feel their eye-sockets. How does the skull help to protect the eyes? What other ways are the eyes protected? How do the eyelids act like windscreen wipers?

2 Borrow a skeleton from a secondary school or college. Find out the bones' names from a textbook. Let the children identify bones in their own bodies, by feeling.

3 Draw around the naked foot, on to paper. Then, using a different colour, draw around the shoe, over the foot's 'print'. Does the shoe really fit?

4 Dangle a cleaned tooth (obtained from a dentist) on a thread in soft drink – and another in water. Test both teeth each week, by scratching with a pin. How might certain drinks be harmful?

5 After eating licorice, look in a mirror at the teeth. Munch a raw carrot, or an apple, before looking again. Why finish a meal with an apple?

6 Use a new boot brush to scrub the thick flour-and-water paste off a hand. (Messy!) How does the activity suggest the correct way to use a toothbrush?

7 Bend and straighten the arm, while feeling what the biceps muscle does on the front of the upper arm and what the triceps muscle does on the back of it.

8 Grip the lower arm while clenching the fist. Feel the cheeks while biting hard. Where else can muscles be felt tightening and relaxing?

9 Obtain a quantity of newspaper, representing the total area of a child's skin, by wrapping pieces around different parts of the body. What is this area?

10 Rub talcum powder sparingly into the middle fingertip. Press on to Sellotape. Stick the 'print' on black paper. Is everybody's fingerprint different?

11 Grasp a polished jam jar. Brush talcum powder gently, where the fingers touched the glass. Brush away the surplus. Examine the fingerprints.

12 Hold a sweet-jar of water, with its mouth under water in a sink. Blow up into the jar through a rubber tube, to see how much air the lungs can hold.

13 Use a 100g coffee jar (which contains half a litre) and rubber bands, to calibrate the sweet-jar. Measure and record an individual's lung capacity.

14 Ask the children to clasp hands, to see whether they are left-thumbed (with left thumb on top), or right-thumbed. Try to find out if the trait runs in families.

15 Investigate the eye colours of blue- and brown-eyed children's parents. Chart results. If a parent has brown eyes, are the child's eyes ever blue?

16 Dangle a metre rule, with its bottom end midway between a partner's separated forefinger and thumb. Let go. How far does it fall before it can be stopped?

17 The ruler gives an *impression* of 'reaction time'. Does reaction time improve with practice? Which child *might* make the safest driver?

18 How far away can a watch be for its ticking to be heard in a quiet room? Test each ear separately. Compare children with adults. Make a chart of the results.

19 Spread the arms sideways. Keep looking ahead. Move the arms forward, until they are just in sight. Now they show the angle of the eyes' 'field of view'.

20 Blindfold a partner, who must then pinch his nose. Feed him little cubes of onion and apple. Can he always tell these foods apart by taste alone?

21 Look into a mirror, to copy a large accurate drawing of an eye. Observe every detail. Identify the pupil, any blood vessels, and the iris.

22 Secure a plastic bag over one hand, using a rubber band. Wait. How does the skin feel? What starts to appear inside the bag? Would plastic make effective skin?

23 Feel with the right-hand fingers to find the left pulse – near the base of the thumb. Time the number of beats, before and after running.

24 Listen directly to a partner's heartbeats. Let the children observe their own pulses as rhythmic 'kicks', while sitting cross-legged. Feel for pulses elsewhere in the body.

25 Put a clinical thermometer under the tongue for half a minute. Read it. Wash it with antiseptic. Rinse off. What is meant by normal body temperature?

Observing nature

The great French naturalist Henri Fabre, self-appointed 'inspector of spiders' webs' and a friend of Charles Darwin, taught that nobody need look any further than an ordinary garden to find miracles. But how many people have experienced the strangeness of watching a dot-eyed plant aphid warily penetrating the hairy jungle on a stinging-nettle leaf? The unfamiliar sight – viewed, of course, through a powerful lens – is both sinister and wonderful. An American professor, Howard Ensign Evans, wrote a beautiful book called *Life on a Little-Known Planet*, subtitled 'a journey through the insect world'. The farsounding name in the title is planet Earth.

How many birds can the children recognise? Have they ever really looked into the minute structure of a bluebell, or discovered that toads have lovely eyes? Observing nature is a thrilling diversion from the horrors of workaday affairs. It is also an inspiring introduction to science for young children. What a pity we often tend to teach the facts of nature common in popular books, as if only they were of supreme importance. *Can we begin by ignoring books?* Children will need yogurt pots, plastic bags and jars for specimens – and magnifiers, to extend their perception. Books can be used later, for identification. Nature is a realm where children can learn by making real discoveries.

Ideas

1 Watch a spider spinning its web. 'Catch' a web on a sticky black card. What types of web can be found? Do all spiders spin webs?

2 Do all spiders 'play possum' (pretend to be dead) when annoyed by tickling with a blade of grass? It is not necessary to hurt them.

3 Where does a web-spinning spider lurk, waiting for flies? Shake the web with a grass stem. What does the spider do with a caught fly?

4 Note whether twining plants, like sweet pea and honey-suckle, climb by winding clockwise or anticlockwise. Do species always go the same way?

5 What animals can be found under stones? (What are the white 'eggs' being hurried away by ants?) Beware of snakes! Don't forget to put back the stones as they were.

6 Find out about the structure of stinging nettle hairs. What are stinging nettle flowers like? (Male and female flowers are usually on separate plants.)

7 'Tender-handed stroke a nettle, and it stings you for your pains. Grasp it like a man of metal: soft as silk remains.' Is this true?

8 Listen near gorse bushes on hot summer afternoons, to hear the seed pods popping. How do these mini-explosions happen?

9 Invent an 'Indian dance', based upon *observed* attitudes and gestures of a certain bird or mammal.

10 In what ways are slugs and snails alike, and different? Find and draw several kinds of slugs and snails. What actual plants do they eat?

11 Watch snails moving on wetted glass. Observe their tele-scopic eyes, tentacles, lung openings – and the wavy flow-ing of their 'gliding' feet.

12 Do all kinds of caterpillars eat the same way? How do butterflies 'refuel' themselves on flowers? Why are some butterflies pests?

13 Count the legs on a common woodlouse. How fast can it crawl? Does it travel straight, or wander? When is it naturally most active?

14 What kinds of woodlice can be found? Look into ant's nests. Try to find the amazing pill louse, that can roll itself into a ball, like an armadillo.

15 Modern birds will use wire and plastic scrap for nest construction. Examine and try to identify abandoned nests. Search them for 'minibeasts'.

16 How high are the stick nests in the local rookery? How many nests are there per tree? Are old nests rebuilt? Do rooks sometimes steal sticks from their neighbours?

17 What birds feed on breadcrumbs? Does a bird eat on the spot, or take the food elsewhere? Notice which birds drive others away.

18 Sink coffee-jar 'beetle-traps' into the ground, in various places. Bait with meat fragments. Visit regularly. Examine catches.

19 Locate a thrush's 'anvil', where snails are dropped to smash their shells. Collect, clean, disinfect and display the hard remains.

20 Investigate an owl's diet, by carefully dissecting disgorged 'pellets' of undigested fur, bones, beetles' wings and feathers found in the nest.

21 Robin sexes look alike, but not blackbirds. Observe the plumage of other male, female (and young) bird species. Are there seasonal changes?

22 Search for trees with bark stripped off by deer or rabbits, nutshells showing teeth marks of mice, and fir cones or toadstools nibbled by squirrels.

23 Identify common wild flowers having poetic sounding names, such as enchanter's nightshade, dog's mercury, lords-and-ladies and Jack-by-the-hedge.

24 Investigate the often made assertion that moss grows only on the north side of trees. What other plants can be found growing on trees?

25 How many prickles on a holly leaf? Examine a hundred. Plot a bar graph of results. Are there fewer prickles on leaves near the top of a holly tree?

Pick a dandelion

A farmer, wanting to stop picnickers spoiling his mowing grass, put up a notice saying: 'Danger – this field is infested with *Taraxacum officinale.*' And, just after the Second World War, a London spiv (out-of-date word for one who makes money by dubious means) quickly earned a small fortune selling saucer-sized bunches of strange yellow-golden flowers with leaves like big green hands. What did the farmer have in common with the street-corner racketeer? Both exploited public ignorance of one of our most beautiful native wildflowers, the dandelion. Its name comes from the French *dent de lion*, meaning lion's tooth – a reference to the jagged points on dandelion leaves. (The hand-shaped leaves employed by the street vendor were those of the horse-chestnut.) Herbalists concocted dandelion medicines for liver, kidney and gut disorders, and recommended dandelion lotion for a skin tonic and wart cure.

The youngest leafy parts of a dandelion plant can be washed and chopped for sandwich filling (flavoured with Worcester sauce), or cooked with butter. Dandelion salad can be dressed with olive oil, lemon juice and a trace of garlic. But the green leaves taste bitter, so the plants should be covered with a forcing pot and blanched. In gardens, dandelion 'weeds' are professional survivors. The flower is a favourite of Danish poet Piet Hein – and its dogged persistence as a nuisance to gardeners might have inspired his little poem: 'Problems worthy of attack prove their worth by hitting back.' If a dandelion's above-ground parts are sheared by scythe or mower, a corky substance called calus forms, to protect the root until new leaves grow. The root is deep enough to obtain water in a drought, and a damaged root can sprout again. As a last resort, dandelions can produce seeds without prior fertilisation.

The dandelion provides a naturally integrated study.

Ideas

1 The dandelion is a composite flower. So are the daisy and groundsel. What does 'composite' mean? Search for other flowers in the *Compositae* family.

2 What is a 'floret'? How many individual florets can be counted on a dandelion's flower-head? Do all dandelions possess the same number of florets?

3 How many dandelion plants are there on the school playing-field? (Measure the area and count the plants in a number of 'sample' squares.)

4 Simulate rain with a watering can, to investigate how the shape and placement of dandelion leaves help to channel water down to the root.

5 Grow dandelion seedlings by setting seeds on damp lint, inside a transparent plastic sandwich box. Observe and draw what happens, day by day.

6 From which part of a dandelion floret does the umbrella-like pappus, a hairy 'parachute', develop? (Is it the 'strap' of joined-together petals?)

7 Compare the growth of dandelion seeds in boxes placed in different situations (shady place, sunny place, refrigerator, dark cupboard, etc.).

8 What percentage of dandelion seeds are viable (capable of growing)? Suggest reasons why all dandelion seeds don't reach maturity under natural conditions.

9 Draw some of the small animals which visit dandelions. (Flowers can be shaken out over transparent boxes placed upon white paper.) A lens will be needed.

10 Investigate the lengths of dandelion roots in different habitats. Observe the recuperation of a dandelion plant 'chopped off' at ground level.

11 What animals feed on dandelion leaves? Search plants for first-hand evidence of small animals actually feeding there.

12 List habitats (hedgerow, garden lawn, waste ground, woods, and so on) where dandelions can be found growing. Is there a relationship between habitat and stem-length?

13 Study the properties of the milky white juice found in dandelion stems. (Does it change the colour of litmus? Can it be used to make a gum?)

14 Prepare and taste some dandelion recipes. Ask an amateur winemaker to describe how dandelion wine is made. Taste dandelion wine.

15 When dandelions are regarded as weeds, how can they be killed? What do weed-killers actually do to dandelions? (Weed-killers are very poisonous!)

16 What percentage of a dandelion-infested lawn is effectively covered? There will be a need to devise a way to measure the coverage of individual plants.

17 Taste French *pissenlit au lard*. Serve small pieces of crisp fried bacon on raw dandelion salad – and dress with vinegar, bacon fat and seasoning.

18 *The Little Cyclopaedia of Common Things* (1890) mentioned that dandelion 'roots are sometimes roasted and used for coffee'. Taste dandelion coffee.

19 How do dandelions survive the winter? Prepare a report (quoting actual observations) on 'Dandelion Survival Factors'.

20 Consult gardening books, learned works on plants, and encyclopaedias to find out if dandelions are (or were) ever cultivated. If so, why? And where?

21 The dandelion has been called 'the toughest flower on earth'. Test the assertion that the smallest piece of root left in the ground develops into a new plant.

22 Dig up a whole dandelion plant intact. In what ways do the shapes, sizes and positions of the leaves differ? Do careful drawings of the leaves.

23 How might dandelion seed-heads be preserved whole? Try cutting them off the top of the stem before drying, or using hair-lacquer.

24 Draw detailed, coloured pictures of dandelions. With the help of a razor-blade (Safety!) and lens, fascinating cross-sectional impressions are possible.

25 Try to explain local names for the dandelion, which include Clock Flower, Wishes, Devil's Milk Plant, Bumpipe, Pishamaloog, Golden Suns, and Wet Weed.

Last word – by a boy (aged eleven)

'I had just come in from outside and found everyone happily munching. But as I put the leaf into my mouth my face screwed up. It was awful. The salad cream wasn't much help either. It was sour and tough. I chewed on it for a while but I just couldn't bear to swallow it. I held my breath and then I spat it out outside. I don't see how the other people can bear it. That was the last time I would eat dandelion, that's for sure.'

Meet Mister Tyrannosaurus

Sir Arthur Conan Doyle, creator of fictional detective Sherlock Holmes, also wrote *The Lost World*, about an expedition to a high plateau in South America where prehistoric animals still survived. This is interesting because scientists who investigate the remote past (paleontologists) have to reconstruct life in the far distant ages from fossil clues found in layers of rocks – just as a detective must construct impressions of a crime and the criminal from a series of less exotic clues. Even small children are thrilled by the thought of monsters, so encyclopaedias for the young seldom lack a page or two of dinosaur pictures. *The aim of this project is to create an atmosphere of wonder and excitement, in which an ancient monster* Tyrannosaurus rex *all but comes to life in children's imagination.*

Inspired by *Tyrannosaurus*, but unmindful of paleontological exactitude, a twelve-year-old wrote: 'It moved on throwing its huge reptilian bulk farther towards its favourite hunting ground. The ugly beast tore up trees in anger as it saw a massive horned brontosaurus occupying its hunting ground. The angry eyes of the Rex gleamed deathly red as it moved into the attack. The brontosaurus turned to see the beastly sight and as the Rex moved towards him he let out a tremendous roar as its enemy fell upon it like a cascading waterfall. They battled on roaring and tearing handfuls of bloody scaley flesh from their antagonist. The two fought on until with a mighty roar the brontosaurus toppled over a nearby cliff. The Rex beat its hard reptilian tail on the ground as if to say who dares to enter my hunting ground.'

We must try to keep within the bounds of scientific plausibility . . .

Ideas

1 Erect upon its hind limbs, *Tyrannosaurus* stood approximately 5.5 metres tall, and was 14 metres long. Make scale models of *Tyrannosaurus* and an adult human.

2 Would a fully grown *Tyrannosaurus* have fitted into the school hall? Draw a picture, to scale, of a child standing next to a *Tyrannosaurus rex*.

3 Did *Tyrannosaurus* stand as high as the average house? Or would the monster have just been able to stare in one of the bedroom windows?

4 How accurately can scientists reconstruct the appearance of the monster from discovered remains? (Study the skeletons of familiar animals.)

5 Scientists agree that *Tyrannosaurus* must have been a carnivore. How can they be so sure that the dinosaur was a flesh-eater?

6 Use white cardboard, set in Plasticine 'gums', to model some 15cm long 'dagger' teeth, with which *Tyrannosaurus* ripped flesh off its prey.

7 Use pictures to help in the preparation of a lifesize cutout card template of a *Tyrannosaurus* foot. Chalk 'dinosaur tracks' across the playground. (Don't forget the tail!)

8 What is the meaning of the animal's name: *Tyrannosaurus rex*? Look up the words 'tyrant', 'saurian' and 'rex'.

9 A lady asked a museum curator how he knew that *Tyrannosaurus* was so called, if it was extinct millions of years before men appeared on earth . . . Well?

10 *Tyrannosaurus* reigned 100 million years ago, and it was common in America. How long would it take to type 100 million separate full stops?

11 Use Vasalined plastic toys, or Plasticine models, to make some miniature *Tyrannosaurus* 'fossils' in plaster of Paris.

12 *Tyrannosaurus* had remarkably short and puny fore limbs which could not reach its mouth. How might this have affected the dinosaur's behaviour?

13 Name some carnivorous reptiles found in the world today. This is easy. It is much harder to think of any surviving reptiles that eat plants.

14 Using reliable pictures, and knowing that an African elephant 3.3 metres tall can weigh over six tonnes, estimate the weight of *Tyrannosaurus*.

15 Make a mural showing scaled impressions of *Tyrannosaurus* and other dinosaurs, like *Diplodocus* and *Stegosaurus*. Did they all live at the same time?

16 With the help of a suitable drawing, using superimposed squares, scale up a chalked full-size picture of a *Tyrannosaurus* on the school playground.

17 If possible, photograph the picture from above, together with the tonnage of actual staff cars equivalent to the probable weight of *Tyrannosaurus*.

18 Create an imaginary tape recording of *Tyrannosaurus* on the rampage, crashing through prehistoric undergrowth.

19 Design a '*Tyrannosaurus* trap', invent a vehicle for transporting *Tyrannosaurus* (by air?), and plan a special zoo enclosure where the animal might be safely displayed.

20 Compile some imaginary advice and instructions on caring for and feeding a breeding pair of *Tyrannosaurs*. (They laid eggs.)

21 If human hunters had lived in the times of *Tyrannosaurus rex*, what difficulties would they have had in hunting and killing the monster? Describe a hunt.

22 Write an imaginary newspaper story about a *Tyrannosaurus* attacking the school. Do it in the vivid laconic style of a tough American journalist.

23 Describe the problems encountered in training a *Tyrannosaurus* (by kindness) to do some entertaining tricks in a touring circus.

24 Paint pictures of *Tyrannosaurus* fighting or feeding. Some of these could show close-up partial views. Check on appearances, using reliable books.

25 Read Ray Bradbury's story 'A Sound of Thunder', in the book *Golden Apples of the Sun*. The story contains awesome descriptions of *Tyrannosaurus rex*.

9
Thoughts on the Style of Primary Science

Primary school teachers would be happier with the prospect of introducing more science into the curriculum, if the subject area could be imagined in terms of a style as identifiable with their working ethos as that 'atmosphere' of secondary science, remembered from their own school days. Style is a characteristic mode of expression or action. The purpose of this chapter is to try to describe such a style obliquely, through emphasis upon three principles. These are: firstly, that primary science should be capable of spontaneity, through a teacher's personal repertoire of simple illustrative experiments and experiences; secondly, that primary science should aim to awaken a sense of wondering open-mindedness in young children; and, thirdly, that the science should be integrated with other subjects.

Instant science

When, by chance, Braille – the method by which blind people 'touch-read' – was mentioned, the resourceful teacher had a brainwave. She quickly found a pin and paper, then pricked a series of grouped pinholes in the material, to signify A, B and C. Next she invited one of her class to come and be blindfolded, before being guided to feel the raised 'dots' symbolising letters. When the teacher thought the child understood what the 'touch letters' meant, she asked the child to 'read' a word 'written' upon another part of the paper. The child read: C – A – B, spelling 'cab' – and told the class. Thus the teacher seized an opportunity for an instant demonstration, needing virtually no preparation, but which effectively communicated a point in impressively practical terms.

Primary school teachers are often reluctant to teach practical science, because they feel that excessive preparation is necessary, and that such preliminaries may demand costly and special apparatus. Perhaps they tend to remember their own secondary science lessons, taught in splendidly-equipped laboratories. There are seldom corresponding difficulties associated with teaching history and geography – or even with art and craft, subjects which can also require much expenditure of preparation time and money. The truth is that most subjects can be taught with a minimal supply of actual objects, and with little material preparation. It is just a matter of applying thought and imagination, to seek and to devise activities lending themselves to instant application. Then indeed a prepared mind can be favoured by a lucky chance.

To be fair, many teachers are not sure what primary science teaching means. Again, remembering their childhood school experiences, they think of electricity, testing for oxygen, or the modes of heat transfer. Oddly enough it is chemistry and, even more, physics that the word 'science' readily suggests. Biology is somehow in a different category – and, anyway, connected in the mind with nature study, presenting no problem to primary teachers. The thought of physics terrifies some people, because it reminds them of incomprehensible theories and equations that in retrospect seem to have been extremely boring. It is hard to avoid the opinion that physics has traditionally been badly presented in English schools; though it is to be hoped that recent curriculum developments will improve its lucidity and popularity with the lay person.

Primary science is, above all, an approach to problem-solving. It involves practising the skills of observing, investigating through simple experiments, appreciation of variable factors which affect a problem, and forming conclusions based upon evidence. It is applied common sense. Through observation a child on a nature walk notices a blackbird consorting with a brownish bird. Further observation leads to the conclusion that the less flamboyant creature is the blackbird's mate – an impression verified by seeing 'her' sharing duties at the nest. If the child believes that the black bird with the yellow beak must be a female – 'because it is prettier' – a textbook resolves dispute. Problem-solving is being taught here, because the child is expected to *watch* birds for answers to questions.

To investigate floating and sinking (during a project study on ships) all that are needed is a bowl of water and whatever objects might be found rattling around in a teacher's desk. Children can learn which solid (named) materials float. Some of the 'lighter' or lower density materials that float can be tested by having loads of two-penny coins added, to see how much extra mass they support. Also, although the children will notice the importance of air space in floatable objects, they should also see that possession of air space alone does not guarantee buoyancy. There are always some interesting surprises. For example: materials become water-logged – and, if a plastic counter is dropped into the bowl, it might be stopped by the surface 'skin' on the water, instead of skimming below.

When children are making and flying paper aeroplanes, a competition could be organised to discover the 'best' performing aircraft. Winning models can be discussed, to determine possible reasons why their designs are superior. Conclusions might only be based on superficial features, or merely relate to the various papers employed, but within such limits science can be pursued. Some children will wish to extend their interest in 'Flying Things', to include kites, birds, balloons and real aeroplanes. *If you are willing and able to accept the precept that process – regardless of specified content – is a permissible emphasis for primary science, and if you have a little courage, you will surely teach lively science as you continue to learn alongside your pupils.*

Harking back to the experience with the Braille writing, the reader is probably waiting for snappier examples of the 'instant science' referred to in the sub-title. Well, an inflated balloon makes a model rocket when released, as it is driven by *internal* air pressure in the opposite direction to its escaping jet-stream. The force of pressure can also be shown simply by sucking the air from an empty plastic detergent bottle. When the air pressing on the internal surface of the bottle is sucked out, the atmospheric pressure on the outside crushes the bottle's flexible sides. A polythene bag filled with air is perhaps the best way to show that invisible air is real. Another way is to invert a drinking glass holding a dry handkerchief, before pushing it down underwater inside the classroom aquarium. Air keeps the water out and the cloth stays dry.

The attractive 'powers' of the ends of a bar magnet can be compared, by finding out through how many pages of a book they each in turn can attract a paperclip. Camouflage can be investigated by standing coloured picture cutouts of animals against different backgrounds. Or a toy racing car can be coasted down a ramp, the steepness of which is progressively increased, to see how the degree of slope affects the car's acceleration and final momentum. All manner of lightweight objects can be compared in 'falling races', when dropped in pairs from the same height. The human skeleton can be explored through touch. And the sun's apparent motion can be deduced through recording changes in its shadows. A weighing machine can be developed from a rubber band. The examples of instant scientific activities which a teacher finds and invents will help other colleagues too.

Magical science

If I am flexing my arms sideways and lightly clasping my fingers in front, three adults pulling my elbows on either side cannot force my hands apart. I don't look tough – so how do I do it? Special training and discipline? There is no time for that. The answer is applied knowledge, spiced with psychological deception – for, remember, I *suggest* that it is the hands alone that are being assaulted. In fact the two teams of people are attempting something impossible under such conditions. They are trying to pull my arms off at the shoulders! The biophysical experiment looks magical, and my presentation may emphasise the 'magic', but thoughtful analysis reveals the explanation. Nevertheless some – and not the least intelligent – spectators might prefer to believe in a special power, however trivial.

Traditionally science is knowledge, and magic is a primitive 'prescientific' mode of obtaining control over the environment and other men. Contemporary science demonstrates a tangible control, illustrated by television, which beams images of the actual world into our homes ('carried' on *non-material* electromagnetic waves). At the same time, official science implies limits to what is possible, relegating alleged phenomena such as telepathy and precognition to an occult or 'hidden' realm, beyond the reach of scientific theory as it exists now. *Yet electrons can be in two locations at once, and pure physics has deduced particles travelling backwards in time.* My point is that the powerful material evidence that conventional science is the only useful route to knowledge should not stop us speculating – and wondering.

Nowadays it is less fashionable to say that an important aim of education is to encourage – or to awaken – a sense of wonder in children. Perhaps that has too mystical a ring for rationalist ears. Stress is put upon knowledge of facts, with less concern for the associated feelings. This is sadly noticeable in sex education. Emotion – at any rate in public – is anathema to a dedicated scientist. A sixth-form physicist teaching the facts about nuclear energy was unwilling to discuss the ethics of their use. There is international concern for the fate of 'Spaceship Earth', where the occupants are rapidly squandering limited resources and ruining crucial life support systems. Teaching science with room for wonder can be of value here, because we never spoil what we learn to love and respect.

My non-scientist students sometimes expect a little 'magic' in our work. I know what they mean, because we have shared experiences with magnetism and light that are indeed magical. It is important to use the adjective rather than the noun, because the body of knowledge called science must certainly be separated from what – for the moment – we call the paranormal. Thought coincidence at a distance exists, and most of us experience it, particularly in relation to persons with whom we have sympathy and accord. Is this 'telepathy'? Dowsing apparently works, even over a map of the area being surveyed for hidden water. But neither dowsing nor telepathy can be encompassed within established scientific theories – yet. To sense something wonderfully magical in science is to anticipate the science of tomorrow.

A lifelong interest in conjuring tricks has always helped my teaching. Conjuring has taught me not to clutter benches or tables with too much apparatus, and to rivet children's attention by not telling them too much in advance. An audience is bored by tricks that cannot be properly seen, so I employ boxes to raise classroom demonstrations where they can be seen by all. It is also boring to watch assistants helping with a demonstration standing with their backs to the class. Other children feel left out. Little children also appreciate my stooping or kneeling to their physical level, where my adult presence is not so overbearing. In individual practicals I aim to keep the activities as simple and direct as possible, whilst infusing some harmlessly motivating entertainment value.

My conjuror's manual taught me that if I had three tricks – one very good, one quite good, and one not exactly bad – I should do the second best first and keep the best for a climax. This is marvellous advice for giving a short lesson with the class. Another vital principle is to maintain clear continuity between the ideas to be communicated. Furthermore no performance with young children is successful without their participation.

Obviously I regard much of our teaching as performance – a means to arouse interest and enthusiasm for ideas, and to influence attitudes. (Yes there *are* dangers.) It often puzzles me that college drama courses put emphasis on dramatic self-expression and theatre, with scant attention being paid to professional competence in teaching as such.

And what of awakening wonder? Let a child look long at a butterfly sunning itself on the school wall, without bothering him by asking its name: that experience lets wonder grow. Naming and the questions can come later, when he will have deeply perceived impressions to act upon. It could be said that the tragedy is that the child will wish to catch and imprison the butterfly. If so, how should a teacher act? A breathing butterfly in the wild is better than a boxful of dead rarities. One living creature followed patiently by a watchful child can teach more of values and the miracle of nature than the finest illustrated book. If dinosaurs appeared in the playground, even the children's never-failing fascination with these fossil memories would be surpassed in a cataclysm of terrified amazement.

Once, during a spontaneous discussion on snails, I recalled with some juniors the ancient settlement nearby, where invading Romans were supposed to have introduced the large edible snail *Helix pomatia* to boost their diet. These snails abound on the limestone hill lowering over the village school, and their white shells, cleansed by brush fire, can be collected there, to serve as ornaments. In fact one of the children wanted to talk about making necklaces with old snail shells. Let us not be too matter of fact about science in primary education. With younger children it matters not how *much* we teach, so the quality of the teaching can be better. There is time to 'sport' a little with ideas, and to cross subject barriers, where new discoveries are to be found in unfamiliar relationships.

Art is science

Integration in education must mean teaching in ways that reflect the living of a full and varied life. I can best explain what I mean with some word pictures.

A boy was drawing a violet ground beetle. His method of keeping the insect still enough for accurate observation was to have it inside an inverted lid of a plastic petri-dish, against a background of white paper. The reversed bottom of the transparent dish rested on the beetle's back. This did not hurt the animal, because, for its size, a beetle is enormously strong. But the boy's patient drawing was coming along beautifully, with 'head', 'thorax' and 'abdomen' in proper proportion, and every one of its six jointed legs accurately shown. The result was going to be a minor work of art, as well as being an acceptable scientific record. Other children were using the same ingenious idea to draw centipedes, spiders and (my favourite) woodlice. Later on, many of the drawings were to compare well with illustrations in the textbooks we used to find the animals' names.

These fourth form juniors were studying animals and plants living in and around the school field. The project began when the children were given yogurt pots, plastic bags and some petri-dishes (used in secondary studies of bacteria) and were invited to explore their surroundings and to bring back specimens of the living things discovered. Of course we discussed the need to avoid damage to habitats, and the advisability (for conservation's sake) of limiting numbers of samples taken. Animals were not to be injured and, in any case, would be returned to the field, when they were no longer needed. Back in the classroom reference books were available, but the children were encouraged to draw and write first-hand descriptions from life. As the weekly Friday afternoon project developed, we produced a lively record in words and pictures. This was integration.

'Project Bridge', as my handout said, was 'a purposeful open-ended problem-solving competition, involving mechanics and revealing (aesthetically pleasing) design principles arising from economical exploitation of a material's physical properties'. The project was devised for teachers attending an in-service course held at the College of Saint Paul and Saint Mary, Cheltenham. The task was to build a model bridge supported upon two 20cm high 'towers', to cross an imaginary river 40cm wide. Only thin cardboard and Gloy contact adhesive were to be used, with scissors, a pencil and a ruler. Time: 1½ hours. The finished model was going to be tested to destruction by the addition of masses measured in grammes. Relative success in the competition would depend upon a 'score' derived by dividing the maximum load supported by the total mass of the bridge.

I have found that, after initial doubts, teachers warmed to

this activity and found the exercise personally challenging. First attempts vary widely. A common mistake is to attempt a structure that simply looks like a bridge. Many improvisations of boxes, tubes, corrugations and cylinders are tried out – and the general effect of the structures as sculpted forms get exciting. Then comes the climax, when the bridges are tested until their 'backs' break. During the testing time we all learn important lessons about which practical solutions to the problem are 'correct'. But 'Project Bridge' does not end there. Next week we have the fiercest competition yet . . . Teachers find that 'Project Bridge' demands more time and actual help in school, but that it succeeds. It is wonderful when we see something like our winning ideas actually applied in the design of beautiful motorway bridges.

Thirty-six fourth form juniors, working in groups around 'tables' formed by pushing together desks, left little room to move about in the classroom. Yet there was only a businesslike hum of conversation. The room resembled a crowded factory – a balloon factory. We were building tissue paper hot-air balloons, to be the climax of a class topic on 'Flight' which had already involved visits to Heathrow Airport and RAF Brize Norton. Finished products, check-patterned, striped or banded in blue, green, white and pink would stand nearly as tall as the children themselves, when the paper envelopes were inflated over fire. This was a lesson in the technology, mastered by the Montgolfiers in 1783, that led to the first manned aircraft. Our operation needed to be well planned. The children (given help when assistance was needed) designed and built their balloons by lunchtime.

This (for me) familiar technical adventure in the causes of science and emotional recapitulation of a crucial event in human history, reminded me of an article that appeared in *Reader's Digest*, in May 1964. It was called 'The Day We Flew the Kites' – a haunting memory from childhood, when busy mums and dads actually downed tools and joined the children flying kites. Francis Fowler wrote: 'We never knew where the hours went that day. There were no hours, just a golden, breezy Now . . .' Unfortunately I was unable to be present when the juniors' balloons were launched after lunch – over a garden incinerator. But I returned to the school at half-past three, in time to see a final pink and blue balloon airborne and sailing towards the secondary school nearby. The children – soon to leave the junior school forever – were thrilled and happy. I have collected children's pictures reporting this happiness.

Some years ago, working with my wife's junior class, we devoted a day to a crash programme, testing a 'circus' of experiments on 'Sound'. Naturally, by afternoon playtime, the children's earlier interest and enthusiasm were flagging. So, after play, we discussed electronic music and listened to an appropriate gramophone recording. As the strange composition of eerie and other-worldly sounds filled the classroom air, the children's faces showed a medley of emotions between amusement and gloom. It was then that my wife suggested letting the children express their feelings about the music by making crayoned drawings. We then repeated the music, until all the pictures were finished – at the end of an exhilarating day . . . The boys drew ghosts, skeletons and other conventionally macabre images – but the girls' ideas were characterised more by poetry and humour.

Was this a *science* happening? Probably not quite (although we did talk about how to make electronic music, using a record-player and two tape recorders). I do not even claim that we successfully integrated the science of sound, with music and visual art. However I do believe that we managed to *associate* the pleasures of doing experiments with artistic expression, during a happily memorable day. Months later, when examples of the children's written records of the experiments and samples of their 'electronic' drawings were on display in college, the department head of English was most attracted by the art work. She praised the lighthearted fantasies of the girls and the screaming horrors of the boys. But what she liked best was a girl's red-spotted, six-legged cow singing next to an acoustically-shattered window, near which was written: 'This is an animal that has just smashed a window and is singing with joy.'

10
Ten Points on Developing a Primary School Science Teaching Policy

Traditionally a subject syllabus was intended to inform teacher and pupil about the factual and conceptual contents of a teaching programme. A subject policy document goes much further in that it reveals ideas about the style of teaching, rationale for the subject, long-term aims, the organisation of persons and resources, and gives some of the ways in which success of the programme will be evaluated. A well-thought-out policy, planned with the co-operation of the teachers themselves, should therefore provide a clear mental picture of how science is represented within the curriculum of a particular school.

The policy will be valuable in several ways. It can be used as the basis of a very much briefer statement for publication in a 'school brochure' addressed to parents; it will represent an essential statement of intent, of assistance to local and national authorities wishing to examine and evaluate the curriculum; and, most importantly, it will provide all the teachers in the school with a practical guide to the content and presentation of their work, hopefully allaying lack of self-confidence and uncertainty about aims. The following ten points are intended to be used as suggestions. They are not a formula.

1 Begin with a simple statement of why the staff believe that science should be an integral part of the primary school curriculum. There should also be a short, clear definition of what the school means by science.

2 Perhaps this will be followed by some reasons why a process (skills-based) approach is more relevant than a traditional main emphasis on content (facts and concepts) – that is, if that is the appropriate emphasis for the school.

3 Now it may be thought desirable to list the skills which the staff hope that the children will acquire (observing, measuring, identifying variables, etc.).

4 Or it might be necessary to set down some broad aims and more specific objectives, under headings such as: 'Attitudes', 'Skills', 'Facts, Principles, Concepts'.

5 At this stage it will be important to think about the sequencing and progression of ideas, in relation to the ages of the children to be taught.

6 Sources of essential materials and books must be considered, with thoughts about the storage and distribution of these materials. How will it be possible to save money, space, time?

7 How will the science work be organised? Will the children all be doing science at the same time? Will groups be working on identical projects? Is a classroom suitable as a makeshift 'laboratory'? What about work out-of-doors?

8 By now it should be clear whether all the teachers in the school will be expected to teach science (the ideal), or whether a specialist, or a special team of teachers, will be responsible. Will there be a science 'consultant' on the staff, to whom colleagues can appeal for advice?

9 How will the work be evaluated from the children's changing attitudes, developing skills and newly acquired knowledge? (A good 'check list' of objectives is invaluable here.) Some head teachers organise regular whole-school science projects on set themes. These are preceded by staff planning, lead to exhibitions and the 'sharing' of results, and are followed up by evaluation meetings.

10 It will be a good idea to give a short list of key books and articles, to which teachers (especially new members of staff) can refer, to 'catch' the spirit of science teaching in the school.

Everything in the policy should be clear and brief.

11
Resources for Primary Science Teachers

Why were several children absent from the class? This question stimulated ten-year-olds of below average ability to discuss common illnesses and the work of doctors. Subsequent investigations involved pulse-taking, making a model thermometer, weighing and measuring each other, simple heat physics and how to keep people warm. The 'case history' is one of many child-centred scientific activities – based upon the children's immediate interests – that are reported in *Teacher's Guide 1* of the 1967 *Nuffield Junior Science* project. There might be a set of the project books somewhere in the school. If a teacher's style is open-ended and geared to children's questions, it would be a good idea to look at *Teacher's Guide 2*, *Animals and Plants* and *Apparatus* – the four books published by Collins, but out-of-print now, although it is likely that copies will be found in the local Teachers' Centre library.

The *Nuffield Junior Science* project books remain a goldmine of advice about organisation, starting-points for studies, and the improvisation of apparatus. *Animals and Plants* deserves to survive as a vade-mecum of what a teacher needs to know about the care and use of living things in school. But many teachers found the 1967 project too idealistic, and felt intimidated by assumptions about their self-confidence in a lamentably unpopular primary subject area, particularly where 'physics' topics occurred. The better known *Science 5/13* project, based on a clear rationale (see the key book *With Objectives in Mind*) and a classic set of educational objectives, has proved more helpful and ego-boosting to teachers. Write to Macdonald and Co. (Publishers) Ltd, Maxwell House, 74 Worship Street, London, EC2A 2EN, for an up-to-date price list of all the 'teachers' units'.

Science 5/13

Individual units cover a large number of freshly-coined theme titles, such as *Minibeasts, Holes, Gaps and Cavities* and *Early Experiences*. They extend the valuable help offered by the earlier project, by giving many hundreds of suggestions for definite activities with children. Teachers are assumed to be non-scientists, while the first aim of the project is to reveal how much science a teacher is already doing through more familiar 'subjects'. *Science 5/13* is classroom-tested, professionally evaluated, and classified into Stages 1, 2 and 3. Respectively, the Stages stand for infant, junior and secondary, although they are not exclusive. The unit titled *Early Experiences* is probably the best book of infant science teaching ideas published anywhere to date; many times reprinted, it has been translated into several languages.

Teachers often complain that the full range of *Science 5/13* units looks too daunting for beginners. True. But the project is not a syllabus. If children can experience some of the activities from only half a dozen units during their primary education, they should learn to be 'simple scientists' with enquiring minds and a scientific approach to problems. Secondary science teachers warmly approve such process skills and attitudes in children coming into their classes. No doubt these intentions still seem utopian, but few would deny their relevance in the modern world. Other units to be recommended are *Trees, Structures and Forces (Stages 1 and 2), Coloured Things, Time* and *Ourselves*. There is also a fine series of affiliated publications, under the general title *Using the Environment*.

Other books

Inevitably there are teachers who feel that the loosely structured *Science 5/13* units are not specific enough for them. They want a more authoritative guide. (The author, who is sympathetic with these teachers' needs has, with another writer, produced a primary science teaching programme (*Sciencewise*: six books for pupils, four for teachers, published by Nelson) that has a structured and direct approach, but still emphasises the skills and attitudes of being a simple scientist.) For infants and first year juniors, Macdonald's *Starters Science* books, written by a *Science 5/13* team member, Albert James, lend themselves to adaptation as work cards. Items can be extracted, pasted on cards, covered with transparent protective materials, and used with 'kits' of apparatus assembled in trays. Alternatively several books can be left open on a science discovery table, equipped with everything needed to do the experiments. Typical *Starters Science* titles are: *Rainbow Colours*, *Powders and Pastes* and *Floating Things*. Well-drawn coloured pictures show activities that are briefly described in a controlled vocabulary. Currently, the *Learning Through Science* project, building on the work of *Science 5/13*, has produced excellently manufactured sets of work cards, based on ideas found in the *Science 5/13* units. (See pages 102–4.)

Equipment

Since work cards are best tailor-made for particular children, it is advisable to inspect commercial examples very carefully, before purchasing. Also be wary of buying kits of scientific apparatus. In general this can be an expensive practice, and the components of the kits may be inferior. Usable books are a teacher's best investment, even if it takes a little time and trouble to gather together all the bits and pieces and essential manufactured apparatus to do the experiments. On the whole, the only equipment that has to be specially bought is instruments such as magnifiers, nature viewers, tuning forks, plastic tubing, timers, aquaria, bulbs and holders, batteries, wire and Crocodile clips, a good compass, and measuring devices such as calipers and weighing machines.

The catalogue of E. J. Arnold and Son Ltd of Butterley Street, Leeds, LS10 1AX, advertises a wealth of useful equipment. Arnold's giant Mariner's Compass is a useful buy. Try to afford pairs of Eclipse bar-magnets. These can sometimes be obtained from larger hardware shops. A *low-power* microscope is essential. Write for the catalogue of Opax (school microscopes), at 142 Silverdale Road, Tunbridge Wells, Kent, TN4 9HU – or contact the county science adviser. Don't buy a 'toy' microscope. Imaginative innovations from the Osmiroid Educational Company (Osmiroid Works, Gosport, Hampshire) include unbreakable plastic mirrors, rocking timers, large-scale nature viewers, clip-together kits for electrical work and an easy-to-use, dial-reading plastic 'stick' thermometer. Always try to see and test samples of apparatus before purchase.

12
A Selection of Useful Books

This is a short list of books which I have found helpful when advising teachers. These, and many others, should be available for inspection and loan at the local Teachers' Centre. The books themselves contain more specialised bibliographies. Reference books compatible with a teacher's personal approach to knowledge and particular teaching style can be found, if some time is spent in leisurely looking around a large, well-stocked bookshop. Self-chosen books will usually be the most useful.

NUFFIELD JUNIOR SCIENCE PROJECT   (Collins, 1967)
Teachers' Guide 1
Teachers' Guide 2
Apparatus
Animals and Plants
Junior Science Sourcebook
   by Bainbridge, J., Stockdale, R., Wastnedge, E. R.
(Collins, 1970)

SCIENCE 5/13 PROJECT   (Macdonald, 1972–5)
27 titles, including
With Objectives in Mind
Early ExperiencesTrees
✓*Minibeasts*
✓*Ourselves*
Coloured Things
Time
Holes, Gaps and Cavities
Structures and Forces (Stages 1 and 2)

Learning Through Science – Formulating a school policy
(Macdonald, 1980)

STARTERS SCIENCE   (Macdonald, 1972–4)
10 titles, including
Batteries and Bulbs
Light and Shadows
Floating Things
Hot and Cold

TEACHING PRIMARY SCIENCE   (Macdonald, 1975–8)
10 titles, including
Science from Waterplay
Mirrors and Magnifiers
Seeds and Seedlings
Musical Instruments
Aerial Models
Teacher's Guide to Primary Science

SCHOOLS COUNCIL HEALTH EDUCATION 5/13
PROJECT   (Nelson, 1977)
All About Me: Teachers' guide for the early years

SCIENCE IN A TOPIC   (Hulton, 1973–7)
   by Kincaid, D., Coles, P. S.
13 titles, including
Communication
Houses and Homes
Food
Ships
Clothes and Costume

SCIENCEWISE   (Nelson, 1977–80)
   by Parker, S., Ward, A.
A programme for J1–J4
Children's books 1–6
Teachers' books 1–4

LEARNING THROUGH SCIENCE   (Macdonald, 1981–2)
6 units (each of two sets of 24 cards and teachers' guide)
    published; 6 more units in preparation
Ourselves
Colour
Materials
Sky and Space
All Around
Out of Doors

Science Resources for Primary and Middle Schools
(Macdonald, 1982)

WATCH – a new way of exploring nature   (Jarrold, 1980)
    by Young, Geoffrey
Book 1 *Signals to Look For*
Book 2 *In Town*
Book 3 *The Garden*

Index